Sensory-being for Se

Sensory-being: the enveloping of natural presentness and awareness in an unfolding sensory moment.

Sensory Beings: people whose experience of the world, and meaning within it, is primarily sensory.

If you support someone who understands the world in a primarily sensory way – for example, someone with profound and multiple learning difficulties (PMLD) or later-stage dementia – you will recognise that they often face periods of time in which they are left without an activity they can access. This unique, practical guide helps you to plan and deliver sensory activities that lead people into a calm, focused state. You are even invited to let the person you support *lead you* into a state of sensory focus. Written by a leading sensory specialist, this book will help you to:

- View the world as the person you support may view it, and identify times when a sensory-being activity may be appropriate.

- Understand how to select and create the most engaging, low cost, sensory foci to suit the specific needs of the individuals in your care.

- Effectively facilitate sensory-being sessions from start to finish so that the people you care for receive the full and many benefits of calm, focused time.

Tried and tested in a diverse range of settings prior to publication, these techniques and practical tools have already helped many people provide an enriched experience of life for those in their care. Throughout the book, you will find numerous case studies and insights from parents, carers, special school practitioners, therapists, research institutions and more so that you can benefit from this broad body of experience.

Joanna Grace is an international inclusion and sensory engagement consultant and Founder of The Sensory Projects, with over 20 years of experience working with people with profound disabilities. She provides training on sensory engagement techniques across the UK and internationally to special school teams, adult care settings, speech and language therapy teams, heritage settings and more. The Sensory-being project is the third of an ever-increasing number of Sensory Projects which each seek to impart the knowledge and creativity required to turn inexpensive sensory items into effective tools for inclusion. In all her work, Joanna is seeking to contribute to a future where people are understood in spite of their differences.

http://jo.element42.org @jo3grace

Sensory-being for Sensory Beings

Creating Entrancing
Sensory Experiences

Joanna Grace

Routledge
Taylor & Francis Group

LONDON AND NEW YORK

First published 2018
by Routledge
2 Park Square, Milton Park, Abingdon, Oxon OX14 4RN

and by Routledge
711 Third Avenue, New York, NY 10017

Routledge is an imprint of the Taylor & Francis Group, an informa business

© 2018 Joanna Grace

British Library Cataloguing-in-Publication Data
A catalogue record for this book is available from the British Library

Library of Congress Cataloging-in-Publication Data
A catalog record for this book has been requested

ISBN: 978-1-911186-11-3 (pbk)
ISBN: 978-1-315-17354-2 (ebk)

Typeset in Celeste and Optima
by Apex CoVantage, LLC

Photos courtesy of Phil Bennett

To
Odette, who left a legacy of awareness in my life, and to
Heath, who keeps that awareness alive. The backers of
the original Sensory Project, without whom the continuing
journeys of the now multiple projects would not have been
made possible.

And to
Noah, a Sensory Being I met only once, but who I thought
about throughout the writing of this book; rest in peace
with your brother, little man.

Definitions

Sensory-being – the enveloping of natural presentness and awareness in an unfolding sensory moment.

Sensory Beings – individuals who experience the world in a primarily sensory way. Sensory Beings can be: people with profound and multiple learning difficulties; people in the later stages of dementia; babies in the first few months of life; individuals with autism whose connection with the world is almost wholly sensory; and anyone else for whom the sensory world is their dominant experience of life.

Contents

Introduction

This book is an invitation to come on a mental journey through the idea of sensory-being for Sensory Beings. Sensory-being is that moment when a Sensory Being is fully present and engaged with a sensory experience. Creating opportunities for sensory-being is not new. Anyone supporting a Sensory Being is likely to already be offering such opportunities – for example, by passing them a favourite object or positioning them so they can see something beautiful. The aim of this book is to enhance and add value to those moments for everyone involved in them.

A team of Sensory Being Consultants gave their advice throughout the writing of this book and through the parallel Sensory-being project which ran in conjunction with Falmouth University's Sustainable Design course. Myself, and the Falmouth University designers, valued their contribution to the project immensely.

Sensory Being Consultants

Chloe

Chloe

Chloe

Daryl

Eleanor

Elowen

Fox

Freya

Gabriel

Hannah

Harry

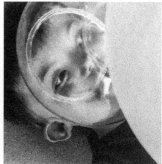

Isaac

Joseph

Julia

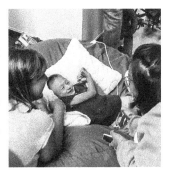

Leo

Lily

Mia

Mya

Rosa

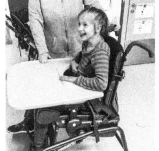

Savannah

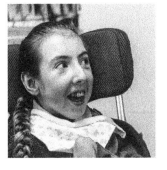

Shannon

Tarik

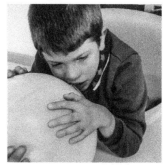

Xander

Zac

Zoe

Thank you also to those consultants who either escaped the camera or were too ill to take part on days when we were taking photographs: Oak, Suzanne and Tabby, and also to those consultants who shared their insights with the team but wished to remain anonymous.

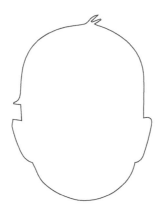

Anonymous

You can access extra insight from the Sensory Being Consultants as you read this book via the accompanying photobooklet available to view online or download from http://jo.element42.org/the-sensory-being-project.

Accompanying us on our journey through this book are a collection of interesting and knowledgeable people who share their opinions and insight in the pop-up boxes that feature throughout the text. Among these people are parents; teachers; adult care workers; practitioners who read the book prior to publication and tried out its ideas; carers for individuals with dementia and autism, and little babies; children with complex needs; yoga practitioners; people with autism and sensory processing disorder; sensory impairment specialists; counsellors; mindfulness experts; Community Interest Company (CIC) members; heritage workers; researchers; artists; and designers. You are not alone on your journey as you seek to better support the Sensory Beings in your care: we all wish you well.

List of contributors

Mary Atkinson	Claire Hill	Coralie Oddy
Leisl Badham	Steve Hollingsworth	Lisa Parascandolo
Sarah Bell	Arthur Holt	Keith Park
Ute Caspers	Anne J	Katie Paulson
Sarah Caudwell	Jack Tizard School	Maureen Philips
Clare Caughey	Mags Kirk	Plush Art Lab
Sharon Cross	Rebecca Leighton	Jess Price
Susannah Crump	Becky Lyddon	Lynsey Robinson
Ralph Dorey	Jo Manuel	Rachel Saunders
Andrew Douglass	Kate McLean	Alistair Somerville
Ruth Churchill Dower	Laura Menzies	Emmie Ward
Sarah Drake	Sally Millar	Gill Waren
Astrid Gilmartin	Emma Murphy	Katie Rose White
James Gordon	Adam Ockelford	

In addition to the people above whose contributions you will find in the text, the following people have contributed with support and advice during the writing of this manuscript: Elizabeth Arthur, Katie Evans, Cathy Arthur, John Aldis, Susan Giuliani, Philip Bennett, Florence Longhorn and Mike Thwaite; the 26 sustainable design students from Falmouth University, together with their teaching team, who designed resources for sensory-being through the project; and a community of social media friends who have cheered me on through the long cold nights of editing. I am grateful to everyone.

Safety

Every experience suggested in this book is purely a proposal, an idea, a starting point. You are wholly responsible for the activities that you choose to carry out. If you are concerned about the safety of any activity, be sure to seek relevant advice before proceeding.

Overview

You may wish to further augment your reading of this book by accessing a bank of photos available to view online or download as a booklet from http:// jo.element42.org (follow links to the Sensory-being project).

In Chapter 1 of this book, you will find an introduction to the idea of Linguistic and Sensory Beings and the benefit of sensory-being for both groups. We will discuss mindfulness and look at how we might approach introducing sensory-being in our practice.

In Chapter 2, we will look at the role sensory engagement plays in our cognitive development. We will also take the time to recognise that sensory engagement and the life experiences of Sensory Beings have value in and of themselves, whether cognition is in development or decline. We examine what choice means for Sensory Beings as we begin to think about the choices of stimuli we will make as we prepare for sensory-being.

Chapters 3 to 8 are dedicated to seven sensory systems, detailing experiences for each that are likely to appeal to Sensory Beings and exploring some of the quirks of our senses. These chapters will be gold mines for any of the sensory work you do. Practitioners who read this book prior to publication found these chapters illuminated certain aspects of the behaviour or responsiveness of the Sensory Beings in their care that they had previously not understood.

Chapter 9 contains discussions on topics that relate to how we perceive and embrace Sensory Beings in the world. Included in this chapter is specific information relating to Sensory Beings in the first few months of life, Sensory Beings with dementia and Sensory Beings with profound and multiple learning disabilities.

Chapters 3 to 9 are supported in the appendices by a series of sensory audits that can be used as a starting point for building an understanding of a Sensory Being's sensory preferences.

Chapter 10 is previewed within the book but has exploded out and is available online as an ever-expanding treasure trove of inexpensive sensory makes, ideas, videos, photographs and insights: go to http://jo.element42.org and follow links to the Sensory-being project.

Chapter 11 looks at how we can sensitively facilitate sensory-being in a way that opens up connection and engagement. We also consider how space can effect sensory-being and how sensory-being can be themed to support different curriculum subjects, cultural connection and memory. We look at how sensory-being can be differentiated to suit the differing needs of Sensory Beings.

Sensory-being for Sensory Beings does not end with a written conclusion. The Sensory Being Consultants want you to know that words are not the ultimate expression of meaning. They conclude the book with their thoughts, expressed in the photographs in Chapter 12.

I hope this book opens up opportunities for both Linguistic Beings and Sensory Beings to connect, to communicate and to enjoy being present in wonderful unfolding sensory moments.

1 Introducing Sensory Beings, Linguistic Beings and sensory-being

In Part A of Chapter 1, we look at the characteristics of Sensory Beings and Linguistic Beings, and how both parties can benefit from exchanging insight. In Part B, we look at the benefits of sensory-being for Sensory Beings and for Linguistic Beings. In Part C, we look at how you might prepare to introduce sensory-being and the challenges of finding time.

Part A: Sensory Beings, Linguistic Beings and the opportunities of sensory-being

In Part A, we are going to look at some of the defining characteristics of being a Sensory Being or a Linguistic Being and consider how Sensory and Linguistic Beings understand experience differently. We look at the value of exchanging insight between Sensory and Linguistic Beings and how these insights can benefit us in light of our differing experiences of life.

Thinking about the different viewpoints of Sensory Beings and Linguistic Beings, and considering our various strengths and weaknesses, begins to reveal how sensory-being can benefit us all.

Linguistic Beings

Linguistic Beings are those who have acquired language, they may read or speak or write. Being a Linguistic Being alters how you think about the world. It also alters you physically: acquiring language changes the structure of your brain and the way information is stored within it.

Sensory Beings

Sensory Beings experience the world in a primarily sensory way. Being a Sensory Being affects how you understand the world; experiences can exist in isolation without association to objects or meaning. Sensory Beings have an exceptional ability to occupy the present moment.

Sensory Beings and Linguistic Beings understand experience differently. It is important that we do not assume they see things as we see them (smell things as we smell them, hear things as we hear them, feel things as we feel them, and taste things as we taste them), nor should we assume that their understanding of the experiences we share is the same as ours. As we share experiences together, it is important that we do not assume our way of being is their way of being, or impose our way of being onto them. Both ways of being are equally as valid.

Exchanging insight

There is much to be gained on both sides from exchanging insight about our experience of life. It is important for Linguistic Beings to remember that sharing insight is a two-way process. We need to spend time sensing as well as showing. If we are resolutely set on trying to teach Sensory Beings to be like us, we squash the value of their lived experience. To try to impose our way of being onto them, or to measure them against standards that relate to us, is to overlook the intrinsic value of their experience.

Personal bias

I am a Linguistic Being, subject to all the biases that entails, so it would be wrong for me to declare that I can show you the world as it appears to Sensory Beings. But I have been privileged to have been close to Sensory Beings throughout my life; I was once one myself, and may well end my life as one, so I will attempt to be the best guide I can be as we compare experiences of these lives.

Being a Linguistic Being

Linguistic Beings tend to be linear: placing their words on a line and reading them in order; understanding meaning as sequential; planning and remembering their lives in order. Linguistic Beings think in terms of beginnings, middles and ends.

Being a Sensory Being

Sensory Beings tend to be cyclical: responding to hormones triggered by light and darkness, night and day, and the natural cycles of the body; processing food or medication as it enters and leaves the body. Sensory Beings experience meaning in the present: they live and respond in the now.

Currency of meaning

For Linguistic Beings, meaning tends to be communicated through the use of words. For Sensory Beings, meaning is communicated in the present through experience. We benefit from sharing our worlds:

> A link with the world of words gives Sensory Beings the opportunity to connect with the Linguistic Beings around them and to know, in small parts without the need for immediate experience – for example, to know upon hearing the word 'home' that they are going home.
> A connection with the sensory world reminds Linguistic Beings that words, which can at times be so cold and hard and inadequate, are not the be-all and end-all of meaning and connection.

Gifts of experience

When we share the experiences of being linear and being cyclical, we offer each other gifts. Linguistic Beings offer Sensory Beings a connection with their pasts and an anticipation of their future. Sensory Beings offer Linguistic Beings the opportunity to connect and appreciate something many of us overlook: the *now*. They remind us that this moment is here, to be lived and enjoyed.

For the Sensory Being

To be constantly in the present, cycling, without the fuss of understanding or the constraints of connection, can be liberating, spontaneous and freeing, or it can be disorientating, frightening and confusing. Supporting a Sensory Being is, in part, about deciding when to step back, so as not to intrude on the natural wonder of their experience, and when to step forward and offer a little of the stability of our linear world.

For the Linguistic Being

To be constantly cataloguing the past, planning for the future, evaluating and making sense of everything can be exhausting. Time runs out before we have finished our tasks, and we feel we have not had enough time and we have lost the little time we had to our busyness. To be offered the opportunity to dive in and explore the round pool of the present gives us back time.

Practicing mindfulness can slow biological ageing

In 2009, Elizabeth Blackburn, Carol Greider and Jack Szostak won the Nobel Prize for discovering that chromosomes have protective caps on them called telomeres.

Telomeres act as a measure of biological age, because their length shortens as we get older. Prolonged stress caused by ruminating and worrying or by periods of depression has a negative impact on our telomeres. Stress and worry cause us to age faster than we would have were we not stressed and worried.

As it is not the events that happen to us in life, but how we cope with these events, that affects our stress levels, Elizabeth Blackburn continued her research into telomeres by studying the effect mindfulness had on telomeres. Working collaboratively with other researchers, she found that mindfulness increased telomere activity.

Spending time practicing mindfulness can slow telomere decay and, in a way, give us extra time as it promotes the maintenance of our biological age in the face of our ever progressing chronological age.

Epel, E., Daubenmier, J., Moskowitz, J. T., Folkman, S. and Blackburn, E. (2009) Can meditation slow the rate of cellular aging? Cognitive stress, mindfulness and telomeres. *Annals of the New York Academy of Sciences* Vol. 1172, Pg 34–53. www.ncbi.nlm.nih.gov/pmc/articles/MC3057175/

Part B: the benefits of sensory-being

In Part B, we look at the many benefits of sensory-being for Sensory Beings. In relation to this, we look at the capacity for sensory-being to be used to turn a negative experience (that of 'parked' time) into a positive experience for Sensory Beings. We also look at the benefits of sensory-being for Linguistic Beings. Finally, we consider mindfulness and its relationship to sensory-being; sensory-being occupies the space in the lives of Sensory Beings that mindfulness occupies in the lives of Linguistic Beings.

The benefits of sensory-being for Sensory Beings

Spending time engaged in sensory-being has benefits in and of itself:

- First and foremost, sensory-being can be enjoyable.

- Sensory-being provides valuable opportunities to exercise and focus the sensory systems.

- Sensory-being supports the development of concentration and understanding of the world.

- The potential for independence within sensory-being counters learned helplessness.[1]

- There are physical and mental health benefits to spending time in peaceful contemplation.

These innate benefits will be explored in more detail in later chapters. There are also pragmatic benefits to sensory-being. Due to the logistics of life, Sensory Beings often find themselves 'parked.' Being 'parked' is at best boring, and at worst distressing and damaging to self-esteem. If someone supporting a Sensory Being has developed a few sensory-being resources or collected some sensory-being items, then parked time can be utilised for sensory-being, changing it from a negative to a positive experience.

Parked

The logistics of life entail a certain number of small pockets of being 'parked' – for example, being left in a hallway whilst someone goes to open the car, or waiting at a door for peers to join a line before moving on to another activity. These 'parked' moments are a natural part of life. It is when people are 'parked' for extended periods that we need to be concerned.

Worryingly, researchers consistently comment that people with profound and multiple learning difficulties (PMLD) are being left without stimulation or interaction, essentially: parked. Simmons and Bayliss[2] speak of students with PMLD being left in sensory corners whilst the needs of other, more able, students were met. Flo Longhorn talks of the failure of some 'integrated' classes, where students with PMLD are parked beside more able peers completing mathematics tasks or writing tasks that they are not able to access. Ayer[3] went so far as to suggest sensory rooms were being used as 'dumping grounds' for students with PMLD. This strong language clearly displays the disgust felt at the situation.

It is not just schools where 'parking' occurs. Writing about the world of adult care, Fergusson and Davies[4] reflect:

Too often providers will consider that simply slowing things down or diluting the content will 'be enough' to mean people with PMLD can join in – when more often it means people with PMLD may more likely be 'parked' there with little meaning or engagement.

A comment on the challenges of parked time from a practitioner

'Parked' time can happen when good people are under pressure. To teach and provide sensory experiences requires time for prep and tidying up that are not always available.

To support and provide a stimulating environment for Sensory Beings on a 1:1 basis for seven hours a day, five days a week, is hard. Staff often request to work with more able students.

Creating a routine way of handling parked time can lessen the prep work and tidy-up time over the course of a week, and knowing what to do to stimulate a person facing 'parked' time can enable staff to feel less like they are failing, making the situation more rewarding for all involved.

We should also note that this staff member finds providing a supportive environment for Sensory Beings for seven hours a day challenging. There are 24 hours in a day. Family members or carers try to provide a supportive environment around the clock as well as managing medical care needs.

The benefits of sensory-being for Linguistic Beings

That you are reading this book probably means you have a connection to a Sensory Being (or hope to form one). If you care directly for a Sensory Being, you are likely to have a good number of things to worry about – and these are not fripperies; these are important things, worthy of worry. You are probably very busy; perhaps working your way through this book has only just got to the top of your to-do list. And if you are putting all this time and energy into considering the needs of another person, then I am willing to bet you do not put a lot of time aside for yourself. I would even go so far as to suggest that when you do set time aside for yourself, you feel guilty for doing so.

My hope is that this book can be a source of knowledge and ideas as you support the Sensory Beings in your care, and at the same time be a support for your own self-care and a source of enjoyment. I urge you not to skip over the benefits to yourself. If you need to justify this in your work or caring role, remember: the people you support benefit from your wellness, so taking time to nurture it achieves two things at once.

The opportunity to spend time in the moment, to enjoy the sensory experience of the now, is beneficial for all. For Linguistic Beings, it can be hard to hold our minds and bodies back from all the other things we feel we ought to be doing in order to focus on the here and now. Focusing on sensory-being is a chance for Linguistic Beings to be present in the now.

Viewing the world as a Sensory Being

We all have the capacity to view the world as Sensory Beings, but once we become Linguistic Beings, we tend to overlook the rich knowing that comes from our bodies, and from our senses, before our thoughts begin. It is a generous act to others when we give ourselves time to be. Like the emergency instructions on a plane, fitting our own oxygen mask of kindly attention is necessary before we can give kindly attention to others.

We can begin in small ways: the next time you make tea, pause in that moment to take it in. Allow yourself to stand still as the kettle boils; hear the sound it makes, watch the steam rise. Notice the smell arising from the cup as you pour the tea. Feel the warmth of the cup in your hands. If your attention wanders from the moment to other things, just gently bring it back and allow yourself to simply drink the tea and be.

Here are some questions to reflect upon in moments to come:

- *How would it be to let this person be as they are in this moment and let yourself be as you are?*

- *How is it to fully bring your attention to another person and to allow this moment to be one simply of looking, listening and sensing to both them and yourself?*

- *Remember a time when you felt someone be there with you. What was that being like?*

Mindfulness is a natural quality of awareness. We nurture this awareness when we open ourselves to what we are receiving through our senses, with friendly interest, as it changes from moment to moment. How would it be to simply tune in to and receive how this moment, feels, sounds, smells, tastes and looks, and let it go?

Susannah Crump: Independent counsellor; Teacher, trainer and supervisor of mindfulness-based approaches; Member of the core training team for the Centre for Mindfulness Research and Practice at Bangor University. www.mindfulnessnorth-east.co.uk

Practitioner insight

I and a colleague wrote a sensory story about a walk. We lay in the park, side by side, listening to the sounds we heard. Afterwards we discovered we'd heard and listed different things: wind, leaves rustling, a bin lorry, footsteps, etc. It was a great time.

Mindfulness

Many people attempt to practice mindfulness, whether secular or religious. The current surge of interest in mindfulness is more than a fad; it is a reflection of the times we live in fuelled by evidence from the scientific community about the benefits of being mindful.[5]

We are familiar with the idea that a person's mood shifts through time; we have happy periods in our lives, sad periods and so on. Less familiar is the notion that as a society our mood shifts with the times, but this is equally as true. Different cultural groups in different historic ages have valued different emotions – for example, the Puritans valuing sobriety and sombreness, or the Hippy movement valuing joyous hedonism. The impact of this shifting esteem for different emotional states is reflected in the mood of the times. Currently we are living through an age of anxiety. It makes sense that in these anxious times, we reach towards a practice that has been shown to counter anxiety.

The age of anxiety

Jenny Edwards, CBE and chief executive of the Mental Health Foundation, stated that: "Anxiety is one of the most common mental health problems in the UK and it is increasing: yet it remains under-reported, under-diagnosed and under treated."

The statistics for anxiety in the UK reflect current global trends, with 22% of women and 15% of men reporting that they feel anxious nearly all the time. This equates to approximately a fifth of the population feeling anxious most of the time: a staggering amount.

Swift, et al. (2014) *Living with Anxiety*. Mental Health Foundation Report. www.mentalhealth.org.uk/publications/living-with-anxiety

Sensory Beings are affected by the anxiety levels of those who support them, both at home and in care settings. We know from anecdotal and research evidence that it is likely that the Sensory Beings we support encounter people who are feeling anxious; for example, research has found that teaching assistants have poor confidence and low self-esteem, putting them at high risk of anxiety.[6]

Living with anxiety as the parent of a Sensory Being

I live with generalised anxiety, and on top of that anxiety I contend with the endless list of worries that come with caring for a child with a chronic illness. Even though I am on prescription drugs for anxiety I still have panic attacks. I lose sleep, lying awake at night wondering how I will get through another day of handling a chronic illness I cannot control, one which could at any time take my son from me. I am debilitated by exhaustion. There is no one else to care for my son, but I have to find a balance between caring for him and caring for myself.

Katie Paulson: Writer for *The Mighty*, Advocate, Blogger: https://withoutacrystalball.com and mother to a child with panhypopituitarism

Mindfulness can be thought of, in secular terms, as the awareness which comes about when paying non-judgemental attention to the present moment as it unfolds. People can practice mindfulness by deliberately paying attention to a particular aspect of their experience. For instance, people might engage in 'formal' mindfulness practice by focusing with a friendly curiosity on the sensations of breathing. They focus on the place in their body where they feel the breath most vividly. They pay attention moment by moment to the subtle details and changes of sensations here. When they notice that their mind has wandered (which is a natural part of the process), they gently bring their attention back to feeling breathing sensations again. 'Informal' mindfulness practice can involve paying deliberate attention to anything you choose.

Many people attempting mindfulness for the first time find it difficult as they mistakenly pressure themselves to become super focused on the present moment, which is a near impossible task as the present moment is always slipping away from us. People attempting to adopt the gentle attention of mindfulness can be helped by having an object to focus on. Experiences that invite curiosity and exploration through the senses are great for promoting mindfulness. A common exercise taught in courses on mindfulness is a sensory exploration of a raisin. People will spend upwards of ten minutes exploring the raisin with each of their senses: touching, looking, smelling, hearing, moving it around in their mouths, exploring touch in this way, biting, tasting and chewing before finally swallowing.

Sensory-being can be thought of as sensory mindfulness for Sensory Beings. The primary difference between mindfulness for Linguistic Beings and sensory-being for Sensory Beings is that, in mindfulness practice, Linguistic Beings notice their attention wandering away from the moment and choose to bring it back. Sensory Beings occupy the moment and so do not deliberately herd their attention. In hunting for or in creating items to inspire sensory-being, we are working to discover objects that delight the senses and invite curiosity and exploration.

Creating objects for sensory-being is an opportunity for you to mindfully engage in crafting, and sensory-being itself is an opportunity for you to engage in mindfulness practice.

Crafting for mental wellness

Like so many people I struggle with my own mental health at times. It can feel as if my emotions are the waves of a tsunami rather than the ripples in water they ought to be. Crafting helps me to feel calm and to still that inner storm. I am a free knitter. I knit without a pattern, and create whatever I create. This means nothing can be done wrong, so whatever happens it is never a failure.

It has been wonderful to be able to create things that help other people to feel present and stilled too. I also bead, tile, marble and turn my hand to whatever I want to try in order to restore equilibrium. Once I have found that equilibrium I can reflect on my tsunami and reduce it back to the wave it should have been.

Jess Price: Free knitter; Support worker to five individuals with learning disabilities and brain injury; Full-time Speech and Language Therapy Student. Jess created many of the sensory-being stimuli used during the Sensory-being project.

The therapeutic benefits of crafting as a parent to a Sensory Being

Being a mum is a full time job, of love and proudness for your creations. The time spent 'doing' for Noah, is not a chore but a pleasure. You don't realise being a mum of a child with additional needs how very busy you are until you look back on the week before. The calendar's full of appointments and meetings; he has a very busy life. Then, on top of that, the daily routine can be full on in itself. I love my boy to bits.

I find sewing and the accomplishment it brings to be therapeutic. I have a sense of achievement that is just mine. It gives me an identity away from Noah. I am unable to work as I am mainly Noah's mum, carer or advocate. I love sewing. It makes a huge difference that it is helping others like Noah. I am paying it forward with all the care he gets from others. I am giving back and it is something for me at the same time.

Sarah Drake: Mummy to two angels: Aiden and Noah. Sarah sews dribble bibs and other practical items for children with complex needs.

Part C: beginning to be

In Part C, we look at how you might go about preparing to introduce sensory-being and the particular role communication plays in this preparation. We also gain insight into the challenges of finding time to prepare from a family carer to two Sensory Beings and from someone who works with Sensory Beings.

When starting out with sensory-being, you are looking to do two things:

• Find, or create, objects which will inspire a positive absorbed focus with their sensory attributes.

• Find time in the day to facilitate experiences of sensory-being.

You do not have to begin immediately. Time spent finding objects or creating them ahead of introducing sensory-being is valuable: do not rush the process, enjoy the journey. In this time, you might also be evaluating the responses of the person you are supporting so as to be better informed about what objects will best catch their attention. Remember that seeking to discover stimuli for sensory-being is not a process of deciding what an individual would like: it is a process of listening to the decisions they have already made about what they like.

Sensory Beings are often labelled as being unable to communicate. This label is lazily inaccurate; it means they are not able to communicate in traditional ways. A person's ability to communicate does not depend on them mastering a particular set of skills; it depends on our ability to listen. Mencap's video "If you listen, you will hear us"[7] demonstrates the importance of listening skills in enhancing communication.

Communication Passport

People who struggle to communicate, using unconventional communication methods, are heavily dependent on others to observe and 'listen' attentively. **They need communication partners to share/pass on to others what they have learned from/about the person so that it is not lost.** *How best to transmit such important information? Not just by word of mouth, as that can get forgotten or distorted. Not locked away in 'Confidential' notes somewhere. The best way is to make a* **Communication Passport** *that goes with the person everywhere they go, that can be quickly read by any new staff or friends who need a 'fast track' to getting to know and understand this person. Communication Passports are usually little leaflets or booklets (but can be cards, an app on a smartphone, etc.) and need to be short and easy to read. They 'distil' key information (rather than listing 'everything') and should always include information about how the person communicates* *(the subtle signs you should be looking and listening for) and how you should behave and interact with him/her to get the best response. Communication Passports are 'what the person would tell you, if they could speak' – including interests and likes and dislikes (food, music, TV programmes, activities, etc.), and information about family, pets, etc. that can help to get you started to engage the person, support a conversation, build a relationship. When you meet a new person, always ask if a person has a Passport and make sure you read it. If they don't have one, try to get one made. To find out more about Communication Passports and about good practice in making and using them, see www.communicationpassports.org.uk*

Sally Millar: BA (Hons), Fellowship of the Royal College of Speech and Language Therapy, M.Ed, specialist in Augmentative and Alternative Communication, and recently retired Coordinator of CALL Scotland, University of Edinburgh; invented the original Personal Communication Passports (first publication, 1993) and now manages the website wwwcommunicationpassports.org.uk

Do not pressure yourself to introduce sensory-being by a particular day or within a certain amount of time. Be aware of who, and how, you are. If you are the sort of person who enjoys rushing at new ideas with full-throttle enthusiasm, then instigate hourly opportunities for sensory-being with everyone and resource them all yourself with handmade items (but be careful not to overwhelm). If you are the sort of person who likes to dabble in something before wading in, then start small and work your way up. Find something simple, like a being-box (see Chapter 10 online) or a particularly entrancing object and have a go, reflect on your experience, evaluate it, try something different and build up gradually at a rate that feels manageable. There are no rights and wrongs, only opportunities.

Caring

Caring for someone who can do little or nothing for themselves means looking after their every need. Life takes on an incredibly focused intensity. You literally have no time or sense of time. You are wrapped up in someone else's needs. Interactions and negotiations with the other person to get those needs fulfilled take over your world. Time loses any meaning as you concentrate on the constant tasks at hand. There are many, enough to fill both hands to overflowing. There is no one else coming to relieve you or offer you a break. You are so caught up in constant activity that hours melt away and there is never enough time. Everything is urgent, yet you have to select only the most essential thing to do next and discard the rest for some imagined time in the future that never seems to come. You are the only one keeping this person going and you know you must not fail in it. Love means that you will do anything for them and by your actions you do. A total investment of your being. Caring is the ultimate lesson in responsibility. And can be an ultimate expression of love.

James Gordon: father to a son with profound autism, son to a mother with later-stage dementia and, before life took over, an information technology (IT) consultant.

Finding time

Finding time is difficult on two levels – in the classroom when you want to have enough time for each student but can only share what you have between everyone, and out of class when you are trying to research and the rest of life places its demands upon you.

To have time to read uninterrupted and then to implement a new idea is near impossibility. We are under even more pressure with a shortage of staff, which is another result of a lack of funding, and leads to us all having even less time. And even if you could counter all those problems then you still need to investigate what the right resources are to research, and those resources need funding. It is just such a long process; there is no instant satisfaction – which is what everyone is after!

Simple, targeted ideas that can start small and grow within all these constraints are ideal. Staff need the time, and the training about how, to watch and listen to an individual's unique ways of communicating and to recognise the subtle signs of someone responding.

Astrid Gilmartin: life skills lecturer for students with learning disabilities.

Notes

1   More information on learned helplessness can be found on page 104.
2   Simmons, B. and Bayliss, P. (2007) The role of special schools for children with profound and multiple learning difficulties: Is segregation always best? *British Journal of Special Education* Vol. 34, No. 1, Pg 19–24.
3   Ayer, S. (1998) Use of multi-sensory rooms for children with profound and multiple learning difficulties. *Journal of Intellectual Disabilities* Vol. 2, No. 2, Pg 89–97.
4   Fergusson, A. and Davies, J. (2015) Future focus: It's all in the detail. *PMLD Link* Vol. 27, No. Issue 82, Pg 33–34.
5   Oxford University's international centre of excellence (http://oxfordmindfulness. org/) is a good place to start when exploring research insights into the benefits of mindfulness practice.
6   Unison (2013) The evident value of teaching assistants. *Report of a Unison Survey*, available online at: http://ow.ly/I7db3027lEU; Butt, R. and Lowe, K. (2012) Teaching

assistants and class teachers: Differing perceptions, role confusion and the benefits of skills-based training. *International Journal of Inclusive Education* Vol. 16, No. 2, Pg 207–219; Edmond, N. and Nayler, M. (2013) On either side of the teacher: Perspectives on professionalism in education. *Journal for Education for Teaching: International Research and Pedagogy* Vol. 29, No. 2, Pg 209–221; Whitby, K. (2005) The employment and deployment of teaching assistants, available online at: www.nfer.ac.uk/publications/TAD01

7   www.youtube.com/watch?v=Hp4PW17U_h8

2

Sensory engagement
and experience

In Part A of this chapter, we look at the rationale behind sensory exploration with Sensory Beings. In considering the bigger picture to our individual sensory explorations, we take in the sequence of cognitive and intellectual development conceptualised as four stages: getting wired, search and discover, explore and connect, and specialising. In Part B, we consider choice and meaningful decision-making for Sensory Beings.

Part A: a rationale for sensory exploration

In Part A, we explore how sensory and intellectual development takes us through a process conceptualised in four stages:

First:
  Getting wired: through experience, we wire our sensory receptors to our brains, enabling us to perceive the world.
Then:
  Search and discover: as we use our functioning sensory systems to search out and discover new experiences, these produce new wiring in our brains.
After that:
  Explore and connect: we continue to explore the sensory world, connecting points of knowledge to one another as our intellectual understanding begins to develop.
Finally:
  Specialising: we set about the task of rationalising the wiring in our brains, pruning it back so that it is efficient and well suited to the environment we inhabit.

Each stage is further illuminated by insights from the book's many contributors and extra examples in the pop-up boxes positioned within the main text.

To gain even more insight from the Sensory Being Consultants who advised throughout the Sensory-being project, read this chapter in conjunction with the online accompanying photobooklet.

The bigger picture . . .

When you are prowling the aisles of the supermarket looking for something that feels like the spines on a hedgehog's back, or hunting through a charity shop for a scrap of fabric as sparkly as the summer sun on the sea, it can be good to have a sense of why you are doing this.

Having a sense of the bigger picture gives a rationale for what can be the seemingly random world of sensory exploration. Having a rationale not only helps you to frame and decide upon what you do, it helps you to value and defend it.

If the most important thing for the person you support is to hold on to, and mouth, a red ball, then you may need a justification as to why they are 'playing' with a red ball in a maths lesson, or why they are 'messing around' with a red ball in the supermarket. Even if this is not an explanation you overtly give out, knowing it can lend a sense of backbone and conviction to your movements and expression. Feeling convinced yourself is often enough to send a message loud and clear, to those who may need it, that exploring a red ball right now is entirely legitimate and justified.

. . . is about development.

At the beginning of cognitive and intellectual development, people fit into four broad groups:

1   Those seeking to get wired;

2   Those in search and discover mode;

3   Those who are exploring and connecting;

4   Those who are beginning to specialise.

Getting wired

Getting wired refers to the neural connections between the brain and the sense organs. People getting wired are often young, but not always. Typically developing children will belong to the getting wired group for a few months at the start of their lives. Other people may spend longer here or live their whole lives as a part of the group. Some people will leave the group, only to return to it later through illness or injury. People experiencing the later stages of dementia may enter the group as their sensory systems and brain gradually cease working synchrony. There is no right or wrong amount of time to spend in this group.

The majority of people are born with a brain and with a set of sensory systems. To access knowledge of any kind, from the simplest understanding of pain to the most complex understanding of a mathematical formula, we need our sensory systems and our brain to partner up. You can picture this as the brain and the senses getting wired together, just as you would wire a battery to a bulb. You need both the bulb and the battery to get light, but neither works to create light without the wiring being in place.

In the most part, beyond around a hundred basic reflexes, we are not born pre-wired. We have sense receptors all over our body, even inside our body, and we have our brain which can process and make sense of information, turning experience into knowledge. Experience opens up the possibility of connection between our sensory systems and our brain. But it is only through repeated experience that the wiring between the brain and the senses is established and neural pathways are formed.

Experience provides the sensory systems with messages to send to the brain. The brain tries to understand these messages, but without prior knowledge, they are confusing. The brain does not know what they represent, what order to put them in, where they came from – it is all a big muddle. Through repetition, the brain can begin to get a handle on things and use the messages it receives from the senses to map out and understand experience. This is where knowledge begins.

It is easy to overlook the work of the brain – to, for example, think of seeing as simply being a matter of opening one's eyes. It is also easy to forget how difficult it was to get the wiring between your brain and senses established so that information could flow. Let us continue with sight as an example of the complexity of the link between our brain and our sensory receptors.

You would not see very well if you had a great pair of eyes but your visual cortex did not function, nor would you see too much if you had a super visual cortex but no eyes. You need both. But having both is not all there is to it.

Have you ever used a manual camera to take a photograph? You have to twist the focal dial to get an object in focus. You have to adjust the exposure to get just the right amount of light on the film. As you take the picture, you must keep perfectly still so that the image is not blurred. Your eyes are even more complex, and your brain has to learn to do all of these things and more, as it not only processes the information received from your eyes, it also sends the instructions to the eyes to tell them how to receive that information: which muscles need to be adjusted, how big the pupil should be and so on.

When we first learn to see, our brain processes everything, not knowing which bits are the important bits and which are not. In time, this changes. The brain learns what to expect; it can fill in the bits it knows already from memory and concentrate its processing powers on the new stuff. When you sit in a room that is familiar to you, it is not as big a drain on your visual systems as sitting in an unfamiliar setting. Your eyes see what is new, or what is moving, and your brain fills in the rest from its memory banks.

What about when you take the photo? Have you learned to breathe out slowly and press the shutter on the end of your breath so that you minimise the shake from your depression of the shutter? When you look around the room, it does not shake. When you walk, the world does not wobble up and down like a bad home movie. Why not?

Your brain combines information from your proprioceptive and vestibular systems[1] with the information it is processing from your visual system in order to understand that it is you that is moving, not the world. You can trick your brain, and experience what vision would be like if these adjustments were not made, by pressing your finger against your lower eyelid and wobbling your eyeball. The world appears to shake. This is because your proprioceptive and vestibular systems are telling the brain that you are still, so the only interpretation it has for the information being received through your jiggling eyeball is that the world you are looking at must be wobbling.

Getting wired can be exhausting

The example above is just a snippet of all the brain does when it sees. It is no wonder that for people learning to see, the act of seeing can be physically and mentally exhausting. It is important that we remember this and allow people the time to rest with eyes closed, or to be in a visually low-stimulating environment in order to have some down time between exertions. Of course, this physical and mental exhaustion can be the same with *any* developing sense, and providing for the need for rest is a very important part of supporting any Sensory Being.

Having the radio or TV on all the time is not a means of providing entertainment; it is a direct route to sensory exhaustion for a Sensory Being.

Sensory athleticism

As I write, I am looking forward to the inaugural Parallel London mass participation sporting event at the Olympic Park in London. On my desk beside me are the resources I have written on behalf of Parallel London which will result in a Super Sensory Race on the big day. At first glance, a sporting event of any kind is exclusive: being only for those who are physically able.

The Paralympics demonstrate that restricting sport by physical ability is ludicrous. But people still think that it is possible to reach a level of physical disability that makes sport impossible. The *Oxford English Dictionary* gives a definition of sport that comes in two parts. The first part says sport is any activity involving physical exertion and skill. Imagine a sports person of great merit . . . you are probably imaging someone who pushes themselves to the limit of their physical ability, someone who asks their body to go further than it has before, to be more accurate than it has before, to essentially do more than it ever has before. You imagine a person who keeps trying in the face of failure, who carries on in spite of pain and setback. Someone who endures until they are completely physically spent, and who then gets up and tries again. Every description above matches someone in the 'getting wired' group as they practice their sensory skills. They are some of the greatest sports people among us.

Parallel London

To many people of all abilities, sport conjures up an image of competitiveness and having to have particular skills. In my view, this is particularly unhelpful to people who have a disability. It is too intimidating; it is unattainable and I think that puts people off. At Parallel London, we place the emphasis on being active – exertion, having a go and being social – the 'winning' is the taking part. Or put another way, the real achievement is participation.

Andrew Douglass: Fellowship of the Royal Society of Arts, Founder, Parallel London & Co-Founder and Chief Executive of innovision.

Being in the 'getting wired' group is wonderful

I have purposefully referred to the getting wired group as a group, not a stage or phase, in order to avoid implicit notions of progression. Progression implies an expectation that one will or *should* move out of this group. Of course, for a lot of people, membership of this group is a stage or phase of life that is left after a relatively short period of time. Those who care about us will often encourage us to move on from this group and look forward to the time when we do (ironically, later in life we then look back and wish our children young again so that we could take in more of that time with them).

All of this – the short time typically spent in the group; that it is a group that most people leave; that return is often as a result of illness or injury; that people hope for us to move on from the group – gives the impression that being in the group is in some way bad. But it is not. It is great to be in the 'getting wired' group.

Being a member of the 'getting wired' group is like lying on your back on the grass, looking up at a perfectly dark sky as the stars emerge. The first messages that get through from the senses and are successfully processed by the brain are fresh; there is no sense of boredom, no sense of there being something better out there that you would rather see or hear/taste/touch/smell/sense in any way.

The moment is everything, and if it is glorious, it is fully glorious – not tainted by worry that the next moment might be less glorious, or dampened by a memory of sadness. If the moment is sad, it is expressed without guilt or inhibition and can end as quickly as it began. Being in the 'getting wired' group is pure experience and expression, mixed with awe and amazement. It is a wonderful place to be.

If you are supporting someone in the 'getting wired' group, you are going to be very interested in providing them with a range of experiences that are mostly likely to register with the sensory systems and be processed by the brain. They are likely to be reliant on you offering experiences. The more experiences you find that register with their sensory systems, the more stars you place in that inky black sky. In Chapters 3–8, you will find suggestions for experiences likely to be processed by someone in the 'getting wired' group.

The liminal threshold of play

When immersed in an activity we are held in a liminal threshold between the day to day world and the activity itself. Musicians talk about this when they speak of 'being the beat,' others refer to it as 'flow.'

The Play Cycle is about staying immersed on the far side of that threshold, in a situation of enough safety and desire that it shields us from the intrusion of the mundane. Play could be flickering ones fingers in a shaft of sunlight or a vast changing experience with a group of friends.

This liminal threshold exists in all kinds of situations from driving a car in traffic to the steady movement of knitting. The quality of the experience is of a perceptual immersive agency. Within play I control myself and also the play itself, if I push too far the play can break. Friends can get fed up. A sensory experience that is too intense for too long will cease to have effect.

The meditative state of creative immanence is important for everyone regardless of age or ability. Keeping on the far side of that liminal threshold requires a great deal of sensitivity. There is no one way to do things. I cannot insist that you play my way. To play you must feel safe, comfortable and desire to take part in the activity on offer. As facilitators we have to create safe and comfortable environments. We must allow people total freedom within those environments. Only when we have provided these prerequisites can play be built by the individual out of the very specific resources we have placed in those environments to inspire the desire to play.

Ralph Dorey (www.ralphdorey.co.uk): Researcher – disability, pedagogy, play, hegemony, power. Member of Goldsmiths Disability Research Centre, former Researcher and Art Specialist at The Bridge School London.

Reference: Else, P. and Sturrock, G. (1998) *The Playground as Therapeutic Space: Playwork as Healing ('The Colorado Paper')*. A paper for Play in a Changing Society: Research, Design, Application. The IPA/USA Triennial National Conference, June 1998, Colorado.

Search and discover

People in the 'search and discover' group get some messages from their sensory systems processed by their brains, and they love it: they want more. Their lives are about finding more of these wonderful experiences. They are star hunters in that dark night sky. They are likely to be reliant on you bringing them these experiences, but they will be active in their engagement with these experiences.

Looking from outside, the activities of people in the 'search and discover' group can seem random, boringly repetitive, unfocused – people may complain that they do not seem to concentrate on anything. Always remember that we are biased by our own position; we are thinking what life would be like for us if we did that.

If we walk in their shoes, see with their eyes, sense with their senses, we discover the delightful newness of the world and realise that the sound of that tin dropping is just as fascinating and as fabulous as the squish of that sofa cushion, which in turn is just as mesmerising as the sound of the vacuum cleaner in the other room and the brakes on the lorry outside and so on.

Their actions do not just make sense when viewed from their perspective – they make intellectual sense too. Hunting for a mass of random points of knowledge – stars in the night sky – gives them a huge spread of knowledge. Focusing in one space at this stage would limit the scope of what they could know in the future. Having a broad spread of random points of knowledge, like the stars in the night sky as we look at it, is the basis of a future fractal system of knowledge retrieval. Focus at this stage would lead to a later linear system of knowledge retrieval. This might not make sense yet, but all will become clear; keep reading.

The Nuns Study: our amazing adaptive brains

The Nuns Study was begun in 1986 by Dr David Snowdon and continues to this day. It is a longitudinal study exploring Alzheimer's and ageing. In general, the Nuns lead healthy, active lives, presumably the best sort of life for avoiding Alzheimer's. Researchers were interested in what happened to the Nuns' cognitive faculties as they aged.

The study has produced many fascinating results, and some interesting contradictions, one of which I want to share with you here: the Nuns involved in the study all agree that their brains may be autopsied after their death. Occasionally the brain of a Nun who, in life, has shown no sign at all of any cognitive impairment will, after death, reveal that she did in fact have Alzheimer's.

Alzheimer's shows as knots and holes in the brain tissue. It is a very physical reality; unlike a virus where identifying germs in the body tells us that the virus is present but does not indicate how significant it is, the presence of a hole in the brain is a rather unarguable impact of a disease.

How can it be that some Nuns had these holes in their brain, but showed no symptoms of Alzheimer's?

One possible explanation is to suppose that because their lives had been lived so actively and positively, in so many different dimensions – service, art, meditation, intellectual challenge, friendship, physical activity, etc.– their brains had formed rich networks of wiring, which meant that whenever a block to processing was found, a hole, there was always a way around it. So although Alzheimer's was present in their brain in life, they were able to function by finding ways around the damage it caused.

Explore and connect

People in the 'explore and connect' group have a set of random points of knowledge that they have acquired during their time in the two preceding groups, and they are curious about these precious possessions. As they explore and examine them, they notice similarities between points and begin to connect them: the colour of the table is the same as the colour of a particular toy; the door slams with a noise that is similar to hands clapping; a fish swims in water and water can be drunk. It is especially important for people in this group that you are providing them with a wide range of experiences but allowing repetition of exploration within this range.

As the connections between points of knowledge are discovered, they are recorded in the wiring of the brain. The knowledge is organised and stored. Picture that sea of scattered stars gradually becoming connected into constellations. (It is probably a little more organised and intricate than constellations, more like the lines on a family tree, or on a spider diagram.) New meaning emerges from what was previously a sea of random points of knowledge.

Viewed from the outside, the actions and movements of the people in the 'explore and connect' group will be fairly similar to those of the people in the 'search and discover' group but a little more focused, a little more concentration displayed. There may be a new element of repetition as people check that red really is red, and that that other thing really is red too.

Here is where the brilliance of that random starscape of bits of knowledge becomes clear. Suppose that one of those pieces of knowledge is the understanding that a toy car feels cold. That piece of knowledge about my toy car has been connected with other points that also feel cold. I have also connected up lots of points of knowledge about shiny objects, and objects that clank or clink when hit. Gradually these points of knowledge join together to give me the concept of 'metal.' When you ask me to give you an example of something that is metal, I do not have to go through every item I have ever encountered, one by one in one long linear line, to find an example; I can drop quickly down through several layers of this fractal network – shiny – clanky sound – cold to the touch – to objects I know about that fit these criteria, where I find my toy car.

If I had started out learning just one point in a focused concentrated way, and then moved on to learning the next point in a similarly focused and concentrated manner, and then the next and so on, all of my learning would be laid out in one great long line. To get back to something I had learned early on, I would have to go back one by one through all my knowledge points, which would be a hopelessly slow and cumbersome process. The randomness of early exploration is wonderfully fruitful later on.

Specialising

People in the 'specialising' group are beginning to deal with the pragmatics of being a part of the incredible world they have discovered through their senses. Managing a whole starscape of knowledge, interconnected in fine detail, is an overwhelming task, especially as new stars emerge all the while.

To actually get on with life and live, we need to streamline the demands placed on our brain. If your mind took in every piece of knowledge available to it as you went down the street, it would be confusing and overwhelming. It is more efficient to focus on what is relevant to you – for example, on where the pavement is and where the gaps in the traffic are.

This specialised knowledge, about what is relevant to their lives, is what people in the specialising group are constructing. Their brains are looking at all the knowledge they have acquired and doing an audit: which bits am I using, and which bits never get used? With this audit complete, a little judicious pruning occurs, dispensing with the bits that seem never to be used. In doing this, cognition becomes ever more efficient; now when I search for knowledge in my mind, the pathways for retrieving it are clean, obvious and uncluttered, and my mind is quick and nimble.

Gaps in your knowledge?

You have probably been a member of the 'specialising' group yourself, but yet do not feel as if you have lost knowledge. You would not feel it, as your brain will have got rid of the bits of information you never used. The precise bits of information that you would not notice as missing are the ones that are missing. However, you may have had an experience of the missing bits if you have ever tried to learn a foreign language. . .

We have 46 sounds that make up the English language. Some of these sounds are used in other languages and some are not, and other languages have other sounds which we do not use. When we were in the 'specialising' group, we learned which sounds were useful for communicating with the people around us. The other not-so-useful sounds were pruned away to enhance our ability to manipulate and use the useful sounds. When we try to speak a language that uses different sounds to our own, we may wish we still had the ability to hear those sounds.

I have had this experience when learning German. Many times I have said a German word to a German speaker and had them correct me; to my ear, the German was telling me that I had said the word wrong but then repeating the word to me *exactly* as I had said it. It is confusing and frustrating: you say, "but that is what I said" and they reply, "No you said ____ and I said ____" – once again saying what sounds to *you* like two identical words, but clearly *they* hear a difference.

An often-cited example is Japanese people learning to speak English who have not grown up in an English-speaking country. Typically these people find distinguishing between l and r very difficult because these sounds do not exist in Japanese. Perhaps their brains would once have recognised the difference between the sounds, as mine would have between the differently pronounced German phonemes, but because knowing the difference between these sounds was not useful in their lives, the knowledge has been pruned away.

It may sound like being in this group is all about losing stuff, but that is not the whole story. What you are losing gives you something. The wonder of membership to this group is in your burgeoning ability to make sense of the world and relate to the other people in it. You are beginning to understand the things you sense and beginning to connect to the people around you. These experiences are not as awe-inspiring as the purity of those first processed sensations, but they are grounding and real, and find their value in being so.

Part B: choosing foci for sensory-being

In Part B, we consider what choice really is for a Sensory Being and what constitutes a meaningful decision in the context of choosing stimuli for sensory-being.

Whether you hope to construct a beautiful sensory-being resource, or plan to grab something to enable you to facilitate sensory-being on the go, choosing relevant stimuli is essential. In choosing a stimulus, we need to think about the person we are making that choice for. We are seeking to have that choice made by the needs and interests of that person, not by our personal aesthetic preferences.

Your first thought may be to hold two items up to the person that you are supporting and ask them to choose. I have seen this done many times, and I would seriously question its meaning and relevance. For example:

An adult leans down over a child who is out of their wheelchair lying on a mat. The adult offers two sparkly wands and asks which the child wants to play with. The child moves their arm towards the wands. The adult interprets this movement as the child wanting the blue wand, the one nearer to their hand, and hands it to them.

Was a choice really made here?

Was a choice really given here?

Making a decision (not a random choice) between two similar but different-coloured objects is a complex cognitive task. It relies upon an understanding of colour, built up over multiple experiences of multiple different colours. It relies on holding a history of those experiences and whether they were pleasurable or not in mind. It relies on an understanding of the immediate future and the impact of the imminent decision on it: that if I choose the red item, I get to play with the red item. For many Sensory Beings, all of this is irrelevant. It is us Linguistic Beings viewing them through our linear framework that see 'choice' in their actions.

It is all too easy to assume, when the child reaches for the blue wand, that they have a historically founded notion of a favourite colour as we do and an implicit understanding that their choice carries impact for their immediate future as we would, whereas in truth, we have no way of knowing from that interaction whether a choice occurred. This is not to say that we should not offer such opportunities, as within the opportunity is the potential to learn that when I gesture towards a particular item, I am given that item. What I am warning against is the interpretation of that response as being a choice made that indicates a preference.

Practitioner insight

This scenario happens many times, with many different members of staff and a lot of students with differing abilities. One student I worked with had limited vision in her right eye and limited mobility in her left arm. Was it better to present an object on her left side where she could see it, or on her right side where she could reach for it?

When I presented two objects on the table in front of her, she would reach across for the object she could see. If I swapped the objects around, she'd still reach across for the one she could see, not the one she'd previously chosen. She obviously had propriocep-tive awareness of her right side even though she couldn't see it.

Positioning the objects so that she could see both at the same time was a really difficult task for the staff, as it was 'guess work.' We tried using a mirror so that she could see herself and the objects, but that added to the difficulty. With a lot of adjustments, we eventually worked out the optimum position for her to be able to see both objects and marked the table so that we knew where to place her seat and the objects the next time we worked together.

We were beginning to see some consistency in her choosing favourite objects when the time came for her to leave to go to college. I often wonder how she's getting on.

What is a meaningful decision for a Sensory Being?

A meaningful decision for a Sensory Being is not made in the moment, by them or us. Decisions, for Sensory Beings, are the fruits of a continuous collaborative process between the individual and the network of people supporting them.

We can think of a decision as being the motive behind a choice. As such, the decision belongs to the person in whom that motive is rooted.

When decisions crop up in the linear world, supporters can make them on behalf of Sensory Beings only if they have acquired the requisite knowledge through playing an active role in this collaborative decision-making process. This continuous process includes drawing on insight from other supporters as well as the essential time spent observing, listening and attuning themselves to the motivations of that particular individual. If you are looking to work collectively to build up a picture of someone's sensory abilities and preferences, some of the simple tools in the Appendix may help.

The Sensorium

The Sensorium is part of the Artlink Ideas Team[1] created to explore the making of bespoke artworks informed by the sensory world of a PMLD individual. My aim was to create a unique artwork for Ben, that would be informed by him and enable him to activate sensory experiences for himself.

Initially briefed by his parents, carers and subsequently by the knowledge of CVI[2] specialist Professor Gordon Dutton. I learned that our perceptions are internalized and that we cloak the world with our own imagery formed in our brains. Gordon said that Ben can only perceive entities if they are uniquely attenuated to his own perceptual abilities.

Focusing on ability and what Ben could do and slowly learn to do, and working over an extended period (over a year initially) I met Ben on a weekly basis to learn from him about his sensory preferences. I created time-based events, mutual performances where combinations of light and sound became spaces where we could get to know each other.

With Ben, we had to slow down time to explore sensory elements of light and sound, sustaining sounds to stretch time and extend his attention. We began to establish our own sensory vocabulary, it became our lingua franca.[3] Our working relationship was based on mutual learning, having fun and slowly gaining Bens trust.

Process was key to learning; working intuitively, ethically, playfully, sensitively, creatively, looking at tiny details of reactions and what might have caused them.

Over many months, I slowly discovered his fascination with changing light projections and high-pitched sound. I became keen for him to have a conceptual and sensory journey that would propel him beyond the physical confines of his wheelchair and introduce him to a rich sensory world, outside of the institutional environment.

For the first time Ben has control. He can control the levels of stimuli he experiences through the [S]ensorium. What this reinforces is that people with PMLD are perfectly capable of learning new experiences if they are given the time and are motivated through sustained interactions. Ben has rewritten his personal narrative and those around him see him in a different more positive light. Much to the amazement of his parents.

1   www.artlinkedinburgh.co.uk/2016/06/the-ideas-team/ and https://ideasteam.org/category/sensorium/

2   cerebral vision impairment

3   a common language between people whose native languages are different

Steve Hollingsworth: artist based in Glasgow; graduated from Glasgow School of Art in 1994 with an MFA; has worked as an artist for Artlink, Edinburgh since 1999; currently a part-time PhD candidate at the Royal Conservatoire of Scotland.

Exploring a person's preferences from a starting point of everything in existence could easily leave you wondering where to begin. Knowledge about the development of the senses yields a collection of useful starting points for finding stimuli that the Sensory Being you support is likely to respond to. This includes people who are losing their sensory abilities, as the experiences we processed first in life become the ones most rehearsed by the mind, meaning they have the strongest underlying neural pathways and so are often the last to leave us.

If you were approaching someone to teach them mathematics, it is unlikely that you would write out all the maths you know on a large white board and expect them to decipher it. More likely is that you would begin with a concept of number, of there being individual objects and many objects, and from this you would lead on to identifying one object, then one-two-three objects, then understanding the abstraction of the counting system and onwards to 1+1 and 2+2, through to times tables and beyond to complex algebra.

For someone in the early stages of sensory development, being exposed to the whole amazing multisensory world can be like being shown all the maths on the white board. It can be awe-inspiring and fun, but it can also be overwhelming and lacking in understanding, connection or meaning. There is room for both approaches in our practice. The next section of this book will look at where to start with sensory experiences. What are the sensory equivalents of the mathematical many/one: 1, 2, 3; 1 + 1; and so on?

Practitioner tip

I read these next few chapters with a pen and paper handy. I had a particular Sensory Being in mind, and as I read, I scribbled down a shopping list of potential resources for them.

It was really useful to have that bullet-pointed list to refer to when I went shopping, it gave a focus to what would otherwise have been a random search through odd shops in town.

Chapters 3 to 8

These chapters each focus on a particular sensory system. Each chapter discusses topics pertinent to our understanding of that sensory system and offers types of sensory experiences for you to explore with Sensory Beings. These experiences are gently ordered into the sequence they are likely to appeal to individuals moving through typical cognitive development. The intent of this ordering is not that you should seek to push people forwards, but that in locating one experience that appeals to an individual, you can look nearby in the sequence to find others also likely to appeal. Look always for experiences that will be interesting but not overwhelming for the Sensory Being you support.

Note

1   See Chapter 8 for more information about proprioception and vestibulation.

3

Stimuli for the visual sense

In Part A, you will find descriptions of visual experiences laid out broadly in the order in which they are likely to appeal at advancing stages of cognitive development. In Part B, we look at sight skills and how our society values sight. We also consider the balance between supporting someone in developing their sensory abilities and valuing their current lived experience. Finally, we consider the influence of money on the quality of experience and conclude that whilst no price can be put on sensory engagement, valuable sensory experiences need not have high price tags. Critical to a positive experience of sensory-being is the choice of stimulus and the considerate facilitation of that experience.

Part A: visual experiences

In Part A, we are going to look through visual experiences likely to appeal to Sensory Beings. Those experiences accessible to the most individuals appear first, e.g. experiences of bold blocks of a high contrasting colour, red, and faces, and those accessible to individuals further on in their development appear last, e.g. experiences of watching an object move across your visual field.

To see photos of the Sensory Being Consultants commenting on some of the experiences mentioned, refer to the photobooklet accessible to view online or download from http://jo.element42.org/the-sensory-being-project. For further ideas of visual stimuli for sensory-being, see Chapter 10 online.

The presentation of visual experience is not simply about finding things to look at; it is also about supporting people to acquire the skills used in sight and in understanding the cultural context in which we see.

Red

The first colour tone we respond to is red. This could be because red tones are the first ones we have practice at seeing. Our sight becomes active in the womb, so prior to birth it is possible that we get to see the pinky/red interior of our mother's womb. Light can be prevented from entering the womb by layers of clothing or fat, so if a mother is pregnant in the depths of winter and wrapping up warm, or if she is particularly overweight, birth will be the first opportunity for sight.

Being enveloped in small red spaces may help to make us feel safe and secure. Chloe, pictured in the online photobooklet, was feeling unwell on the day we visited her. She was unresponsive to other stimulus and looked anxious and upset. However, hidden in the small red world of the umbrella, she appeared calm and focused.

Faces

We are born with around a hundred reflexes; each is a little piece of pre-wiring in the brain aimed at ensuring our survival. One of these many reflexes is for faces. Our eyes are instinctively, reflexively drawn to the faces around us. Looking at the faces of those around is a good way for an infant to connect with the people who are likely to protect it and ensure its survival. Some of our reflexes wear off in the first few months of life; the face reflex remains with us throughout life.

The person you support is likely to enjoy looking at faces. Position yourself so they can see your face clearly and easily; hold your face level with and close to theirs. Looking in a mirror together is a way of doing this that feels less intrusive. A mirror is a great and simple way to enable a Sensory Being to look at their own face. Objects with faces on may be more interesting than objects without faces. Even the simplest of doodles, just eyes and a mouth in marker pen, can serve to make an object more visually fascinating.

As well as knowing that Sensory Beings may appreciate faces for their visual interest, it is also worth being aware of the pressure faces in the environment can pose for some people. Individuals with autism can find looking at a person's face stressful, yet their eyes may be reflexively drawn to faces in the room. Thinking about the space you are in can be useful; for example, someone in need of a visual break is unlikely to find a room full of faces a restful environment. A room with lots of portraits on the wall is a very different visual environment to a room with lots of pictures of trees on the wall, even if the pictures in both rooms are of a similar vibrancy.

High contrast

As with all our senses, in order to function our brain must work in conjunction with the associated sensory systems to make sense of the information presented. The difference between a signal saying "this is bright" and one saying "this is dark" is easier to interpret than the difference between two signals describing pale peach and lemon yellow. It makes sense that early in the development of sight, we find it easiest to respond to high-contrast visuals. Look for clear black-and-white images with bold blocks of colour. It is not as simple as finding black-and-white images. If the blocks of colour are not bold enough, the brain may get confused about the locations of the separate colours; for example, black lines on a white page may be seen as a grey blur.

Backgrounds

High-contrast visuals do not have to be black and white; for example, a large, bright-red circle presented on a soft-yellow background would be visually easy to pick out. Considering the background to an object that you hope will be seen by a Sensory Being is enormously important in making the sight experience you are offering them accessible. An individual may be able to see a black pen held on a white piece of paper but unable to see it in a pile of other pens. Be aware that shiny surfaces do not keep true to the colour that they are. For example, a black tray may seem like a super opportunity for presenting white objects; however, if the tray has a gloss finish, the visual experience presented could be a reflection of the ceiling, the light fittings, your arms and chin as you extend the tray, and somewhere within that muddle the white object which you assumed was being presented against a highly contrasting background.

Personal

Each individual is different, and their early experiences are different. A child who spent its first months of life in an incubator is going to have experienced a very different visual environment to a child who spent its first months of life carried in a sling. These differing visual environments provide different experiences for the brain to practice its understanding on, and these in turn lead to different visual skills and preferences. One of the best things you can do when supporting someone to see is to notice what their vision is drawn to. Keep a mental note, or better still a physical one, of what colours they respond to, and whether they respond more in bright or dull environments and so on. The sensory audits in the Appendix can be a useful starting point in beginning to think about what someone else sees.

Light

Light is electromagnetic radiation. The visible wavelengths of electromagnetic radiation are known to us as colours (other animals can see more of the spectrum than us, so they arguably have a broader palette of colours). When light hits a surface, some of it is absorbed as energy, warming the surface, and some of it is bounced back. What is bounced back is determined by what colour the surface is. A red surface bounces back light from the 'red' wavelength section of the electromagnetic spectrum. Put simply: colour is light; without light there is no sight. This means lighting is going to be monumentally important when you are considering how to support someone to see.

Correct lighting plays a huge role in ensuring an object is visible. Consider using a small pen torch to pick an object out from its surroundings and make it more visible for the person you are supporting. Be aware that making an object too bright can make it hard to look at, and that objects that are shiny may reflect a light source directly, creating a bright point on the object that eclipses the rest of it.

You may have had an experience taking a photo where a bright object in the image threw the balance of the whole picture out in such a way that you could not see anything else. Or on a particularly bright day, you may have momentarily been blinded by the glare of an object. If you offer someone a bright point of light to look at (like the end of your torch), they may connect with it and stare at it. This can look like success, as you have secured their engagement with the visual world, but it very quickly becomes a dead end as it serves to block out everything else.

There are simple ways of diffusing light so that you can offer the benefit of its brightness but not have it all focused in one place; for example, use tracing paper or baking paper laid over a light source to soften the glare, or place a light source inside something frosted – even something simple like a plastic milk carton can work. See online content for an example of a simple light-diffusing sensory make.

Fluorescent colours

Fluorescent colours are much brighter than ordinary colours, as when light hits them, they bounce back not only the parts of the electromagnetic spectrum that relate to the visible colours we know, the ones we sing about in the rainbow song, but also other parts of the spectrum. In essence, they send more light to our eyes, making them appear brighter. The Sensory Being you support may find it easier to spot fluorescent colours. Consider presenting them against a plain contrasting background, preferably one that is matt.

UV light

Ultraviolet (UV) light is not visible to the general population. However, when we shine UV light onto something fluorescent, something wonderful happens: it changes into visible light and is reflected back to us at wavelengths we can perceive. This means that using UV lighting to light an object is a way of adding extra light to a visual experience. As vision is reliant on light entering the eye, by giving a person more light to see, we are increasing the information sent from their eyes to their brain. For some people, this strengthening of the signal will enable them to see something that they otherwise would not have been able to see.

When we use UV lighting in a room that is otherwise dark, it appears magic, as we cannot see the light landing on the objects but we can see it when it bounces off them; consequently, fluorescent objects appear to glow.

When we use UV lighting in a lit room (whether that room is lit by natural or artificial light), we are bringing extra light to the environment which fluorescent objects will reflect back to us, making them appear brighter.

Small UV pen torches cost as little as £1–£3 and are a good way of picking out an object for a person to focus on. UV light bulbs can be purchased for around £5–£10 and used to fluoresce a whole room.

Static seeing

We know vision is not simply something that happens. We know there are two parts to the process: the retrieval of the information from the world, and the processing of that information by the brain. In the introduction to this chapter of the book, I talked about some of the complexities of seeing as an example of how many skills are involved in sensing. So far in this chapter, I have been discussing vision as if everything is static: ourselves and the things we look at. But it is not. Think about all the skills involved in retrieving information from the environment when we add movement into the mix. Because movement makes seeing more complex, many Sensory Beings will find it tricky to see an object that moves across their field of vision. However, wiggling an object slightly whilst keeping it in the same location in the visual field will make it more visually interesting, as it stimulates more visual receptors than a stationary object without the added demand of asking the eye to track it as it moves from one position to another.

Movement

Seeing a moving object requires extra skills from the body, as it is called upon to control the muscles around our eyes which turn and focus the eye. However, different parts of the eye are responsible for registering shape and colour and movement. So when an object moves, messages are sent about shape, colour AND movement. In other words, a moving object provides extra stimulation. This means that moving objects can be more visually interesting. However, if you are not able to follow an object's movement, as many Sensory Beings are not, then a moving object is simply one you were able to see, but then it moved and vanished.

It is possible that particular conditions or complexities of brain injury could result in a person struggling to see shape and colour but being able to see movement. For such a person, a moving stimulus would be easier to see. As someone supporting a Sensory Being, it is down to you to do the detective work, watching their responses and reactions to see which sort of visual stimulus they enjoy the most.

Patterns

Certain visual experiences and patterns appear particularly interesting to the eyes. This is reflective of the way the sensors are arranged on our retinas. People who experience drug-induced hallucinations often report seeing things like spirals or tunnels. These hallucinations are a result of the arrangement of our visual sensors. Exploring spirals, spinning concentric circles, or geometric patterns, checker boards, and lattices can be particularly interesting to the eyes. Colouring in these patterns could be a lovely way for you and the person you support to enjoy collaborative sensory-being.

Distance

When trying to look at an object, we need to control the movements of the muscles around our eyes to focus our eyes on that object. Looking at an object near to us is a different visual skill to looking at one far away. When we are first seeing, we may find it hard to stretch our eyes to a focal point in the distance. It is more likely that we will see at the distance our eyes naturally settle. The precise distance best for those in the early stages of the development of sight is going to be different for each individual, but it is likely to be quite close up: a forearm's length away or the length of the long side of a sheet of A4 paper. For this reason, you may find the person you support responds better to visual stimuli that are presented quite close to them.

Sensory umbrellas

Sensory umbrellas, an idea from Flo Longhorn and Richard Hirstwood, are a great way to present a clear visual stimulus against a close-up, high-contrast matt background. See Figure 10.3.5 for an example. It is one of many in my brolly arsenal. Once you start making them, it is hard to walk past a good umbrella without buying it to turn into a small sensory world – see online for more information (http://jo.element42.org).

Take-away tips

- Always think about the visual environment around the object you are offering as a focal point for visual stimulation as well as about the properties of the object itself.

- Think about the processing demands placed on a Sensory Being's visual systems by the experience you are offering. Moving stimuli require more processing, bright colourful backgrounds require more processing than dark matt backgrounds, and so on.

- Make use of faces and be aware that faces and spinning are especially visually interesting.

Part B: visual skills and the valuing of the visual world

The presentation of visual experience is not simply about finding things to look at; it is also about supporting people to acquire the skills used in sight and in understanding the cultural context in which we see. In Part B, we look at sight skills and how our society values sight. We also consider the balance between supporting someone in developing their sensory abilities and valuing their current lived experience. Finally, we consider the influence of money on the quality of experience and conclude that whilst no price can be put on sensory engagement, valuable sensory experiences need not have high price tags. Critical to a positive experience of sensory-being is the choice of stimulus and the considerate facilitation of that experience.

Sight skills

Beyond establishing the connection between the brain and the senses, there are many other skills to acquire with sight. Learning to control the muscles around our eyes in order to enable us to focus at different distances, as discussed above, is just one of a multitude of skills. We also learn to control our eyes so they can track objects across our field of vision, to jump our eyes from one object to another and back, to hunt around our visual field for a particular object, to scan methodically and so on.

Acquiring visual dexterity requires a great deal of practice and dedication. If you are supporting a Sensory Being undertaking these challenges, you can help them to meet these challenges by offering them clear visual experiences in graded steps. For example, if you are looking to support someone meeting the challenge of following a moving object with their sight, you are not going to start by asking them to follow the movements of a squash ball in a squash game.

You are going to start by showing them a bright, clear object moving steadily from one side of their visual field to the other, and you are going to do that *a lot*, so they have many chances to practice their new skill. You might move on to showing them an object moving steadily up and down. Or you might move on to an object moving at slightly different speeds so that it tracks slowly across their field of vision, then speeds up for a bit, then slows down again.

Teaching Hugh to see

Hugh is a happy smiley little boy with an entirely unique chromosomal translocation (he is the only person in the world with his chromosomal arrangement), which means he leads a medically complex life. One of the many impacts of Hugh's chromosomal translocation is that Hugh was born blind. Despite the diagnosis of blindness being one of a long list – developmental delay, seizures, hypotonia and feeding difficulties, to mention a few – the people who care for Hugh were not about to let it lie: they began a process of teaching Hugh to see.

> We borrowed a dark den – a huge tent that blocks out all the light – and I'd sit in there endlessly with light up bouncing balls and fibre optics trying to **teach** him to see.
> Emma Murphy: mother to Hugh @HappyLittleHugh – extract
> from "Seeing and believing," *Little Mama Murphy* (blog),
> 11 November 2015. Read the full story at: www.littlemamamurphy.
> co.uk/2015/11/seeing-and-believing.html

[Spoiler alert – the post ends with Hugh trying on glasses!]

Society values sight

Our senses are valued against the world we inhabit. There is no natural hierarchy, but we have developed a world that holds vision in very high regard, so there are many visual skills that we are expected to master in order to access that world. You are probably using one of them right now as you scan from left to right along these lines of little black squiggles onto which our society bestows meaning. What an exceptional act of visual precision this is, to look at these tiny similar squiggles in order and to keep your place on the page when there are so many other similar squiggles all around.

Practitioner question

If we have developed the world to be sight-dominated, what is to stop us from developing classrooms that are a different way? What about an auditory way? An olfactory way? A multisensory way?

This sight-dominated world can make us think that vision is particularly complex, but it is not. We have just paid particular attention to its complexity. Were we to pay the same attention to any of our other senses, we would discover the same wonderful potential for skilled use.

Shopping for development?

Hopefully, whilst reading this chapter, you have begun to create a list of ideas for resources you might try with the person you are supporting. A shopping list is a good place for a Linguistic Being to start their adventures into the sensory world. Your list is likely to be in the developmental order that the ideas were presented in the book. Be careful: thinking about development can be a slippery slope, because our linear nature means that when we think of 'starts,' we automatically move on to thinking of 'middles' and 'ends' as well. And as we shop for these 'starting' experiences, we are already thinking of where these experiences might take us.

Linguistic Beings drive their attention along the line of development so that their focus ends up wholly at the end point. The problem with this is it misses the now. We need to use the list to think three-dimensionally. Not: What is next? But: What else is now? The person you support is at a particular point on that line of development: What is around them at that point? What are the experiences to be had and enjoyed in the here and now?

Understanding the development of the senses is not about forcing development to happen faster, it is about finding connection in the now.

Chimeabout

A Chimeabout is a wooden toy that looks like a carousel. From each of its five wooden arms, long thin mirrors with colourful backings hang. Each mirror has a bell attached with a keyring fastening. It can be spun, causing the mirrors to fly out and the bells to jingle. It is a fantastically engaging sensory item. When I mentioned it on social media, I instantly received a flood of testimony from parents and practitioners who had shared the toy with Sensory Beings. Here is a taste of that deluge of praise:

> The Chimeabout is great for pupils who respond to sound. In my current class I have a little girl with limited arm movement who will happily interact with the Chimeabout for the whole of lunch break. This little girl often smiles in response to other stimuli but rarely reaches out to interact with them in the way that she does with the Chimeabout.
>
> Leisl Badham: SEND (special educational needs and disabilities)
> Class teacher and Science lead

My son Hugh is a medical mystery full of smiles. The Chimeabout was his favourite toy for a long time. It was the only thing he responded to consistently in the early days.
Emma Murphy: mother to Hugh. www.littlemamamurphy.co.uk,
@HappyLittleHugh

The Chimeabout is great for attracting the attention of people who may require an auditory prompt to support the visual context, encouraging reaching and grasping. I have noticed opportunities for lots of intense visual attention to the mirrors, pulling them closer and the bells have supported the students grasping the mirror. You obviously have to watch people who explore with their mouths. I like to have them on a sunny windowsill personally, so that the sun then bounces on the walls and the wind can cause the bells to sound!
Anne, J.: higher level teaching assistant (HLTA) in a SEND School, Shropshire

There is a girl in my class who absolutely loves the Chimeabout toys. She has profound visual impairment and very limited hand movement but with the Chimeabout she can have a sensory experience independently with only the slightest movement from her.
Sarah Caudwell: Special School Class teacher

In my experience Chimeabouts attract everyone's attention (regardless of age and ability). It's like magpies to shiny things. They make a fabulous jingle as they spin and the mirrors and colours provide all sorts of visual stimulation. I haven't met a child yet that didn't love them.
Rachel Saunders: special educational needs (SEN) teacher,
Carlton Digby School, Nottingham

I once had a child who refused to eat at all unless a member of staff repeatedly chimed a Chimeabout in the background!
Dr Clare Caughey: Educational Psychologist and Consultant,
Founder of SENsations Learning Support CIC,
www.sensationsni.co.uk

Noise, light and touch rolled into hours of sensory enjoyment.
Sarah Drake: Mummy to two angels: Aiden and Noah

What is it about this simple toy that so unites people supporting Sensory Beings? I expect you already have a few ideas. This toy ticks so many early developmental sensory boxes: jangly sounds; spinning; the opportunity to see oneself and the faces of others; light framed against dark, bright contrasting colours; movement. Add to that its ease of use – even a small movement gets rewarded with a big sensory response – and you know you are onto a winner.

Some commentators go on to mention that Chimeabouts are expensive. Although undoubtedly worth it if you can afford it, sensory magic does not have to be expensive. Another hugely popular item, and perfect opportunity for sensory-being, is a section of space blanket. Where a Chimeabout costs over £50, a space blanket is a little over 50p.

What price engagement?

The price of the product does not determine how effective it will be at engaging a person. Two things are important when choosing sensory experiences for a Sensory Being:

- Knowledge of what types of experiences are likely to engage them.

- Knowledge about how to facilitate those experiences.

With knowledge about what experiences are likely to engage, you can find items to buy for thousands of pounds or for a few pence that will delight their senses. With knowledge about how to facilitate sensory experiences successfully, you will be able to use these items to connect with Sensory Beings and enrich their world. Without this knowledge, you can waste loads of money on useless items or have the most fabulous piece of kit and achieve nothing with it.

Research highlights the importance of stimulus choice and facilitation

Reflecting on earlier studies,[1] a team of researchers[2] interested in the impact of staff interaction style during multisensory storytelling report that studies "have demonstrated that sensory stimulation sessions in which preferred objects are used and staff pay extensively attention to the interaction with the person with PIMD,[3] lead to the same or even better results (e.g. alertness, active behaviours towards stimuli) than comparable activities in specifically designed and expensive multisensory rooms where there is less focus on social interaction."

[1] Fava, L. and Strauss, K. (2010) Multi-sensory rooms: comparing effects of the Snoezelen and the Stimulus Preference environment on the behavior of adults with profound mental retardation. *Research in Developmental Disabilities* Vol. 31, No. 1, Pg 160–171. doi: 10.1016/j.ridd.2009.08.006. Epub 2009 Oct 7.

Lancioni, G. E., Cuvo, A. J. and O'Reilly, M. F. (2002) Snoezelen: an overview of research with people with developmental disabilities and dementia. *Disability and Rehabilitation* Vol. 24, Pg 175–184.

Vlaskamp, C., De Geeter, K. I., Huijsmans, L. M. and Smit, I. H. (2003) Passive activities: the effectiveness of multisensory environments on the level of activity of individuals with profound multiple disabilities. *Journal of Applied Research in Intellectual Disabilities* Vol. 16, Pg 135–143.

[2] Penne, A., Ten Brug, A., Munde, V., van der Putten, A., Vlaskamp, C. and Maes, B. (2012) Staff interactive style during multisensory storytelling with persons with profound intellectual and multiple disabilities. *Journal of Intellectual Disability Research* Vol. 56, No. 2, Pg 167–178.

[3] PIMD stands for profound intellectual and multiple disabilities. In the UK, these people would be considered to have PMLD (profound and multiple learning difficulties). People with PIMD or PMLD would be Sensory Beings.

Take-away tips

- Sight, the process of seeing, is a very skilled business requiring the co-ordination of mind and body. Acquiring this co-ordination takes practice. Support Sensory Beings in getting this practice by repeating experiences multiple times.

- We live in a visually dominated society, meaning we naturally acquire a visual bias. Remember, the Sensory Being/s you support may have a different dominant sense.

- Trying to force a person's development is counterproductive. Look for a range of experiences that relate to the person's current developmental state and allow them time to enjoy and process them fully.

- Expensive equipment is not always best. The most important thing is to have the relevant knowledge to enable you to choose experiences to suit the Sensory Being you are supporting.

4

Stimuli for the olfactory sense

This chapter begins with an examination of the value of our olfactory sense and a consideration of how many sensory systems we have.

In Part B, we look at how our olfactory sense develops and what experiences are likely to appeal to Sensory Beings as they begin their adventures with smell.

In Part C, we continue to explore olfactory experiences likely to interest Sensory Beings and how to facilitate these for maximal benefit as we consider how we take in and process the smells in our environment.

Part A: the olfactory sense; one of many fascinating senses

Our olfactory sense of smell is an undervalued sense. Often, we do not realise what it brought to our lives until it is gone. In Part A, we look at the role our olfactory sense plays in our lives over and above the obvious one of telling us what things smell like. This leads us to an interesting tangent in the second part of Part A, as we consider how many senses we truly have: is it 5, is it 7, 9, 11, or even 33?

Like all senses, smell has a development. But, because it is not a sense we value as highly as some, we are not so prone to thinking of it as a linear sequence of achievements. You may have overheard a parent proudly declaring their child can identify certain colours. Have you ever overheard a parent declaring what scents their child can identify?

Survival value

Historically our sense of smell would have been a valuable tool for keeping us safe: we would have smelt out food to eat; we would have sniffed food to check whether it was off; we would have smelt sickness in others and avoided them. Today, if you put a dish of food down before me in a restaurant that smelt a bit funny, I would be just as likely to override my instincts and assume the scent was the chef's intention as to send it back to the kitchen.

Smell would also have played a role in how we chose a mate. It still does. We tend to prefer the smell of people with whom we are genetically compatible. I doubt you feel like you are choosing a partner based on scent, but you would be unlikely to partner with someone whom you did not like the smell of. If you have friends open to a little sensory exploration, try sniffing the crowns of people's heads; mostly likely they will all smell fine, but your partner's head will smell wonderful.

Determining life through scent

Certain smells will set you on edge – smells that remind you of unpleasant or frightening occasions. Other smells might comfort you or remind you of a loved one. But, in the main, I expect that smell plays a relatively background role in your life. But just because smell falls into the background of our experience does not mean that it does for Sensory Beings.

Smells can be a source of anxiety, fear or even pain.

Emotions

Smell is processed by the limbic brain, our emotional brain. Our other senses are processed by the thalamus, the thinking brain. Smell is therefore a particularly emotional and emotive sense. Smells that frighten us and smells that comfort us are more powerful than a stimulus from another sense we find frightening or pleasing.

Memory

With its strong connection to our emotions, smell is a powerful tool in memory. A Sensory Being may not remember an event in the same storytelling way that we do, i.e. that once they were here before and they had a particular experience. Their sense of smell may connect them with memories in an instantaneous way: they smell that hospital smell and instantly feel the same emotions they felt last time they smelled that smell.

Pain

We have two types of olfactory receptors in our nasal passageways: ones for volatile scents, and ones for pheromone scents. We also have receptors from our somatosensory system. The somatosensory system is dedicated to the sensation of temperature, pressure and pain.

For pragmatic reasons as I run the Sensory Projects, I focus on seven sensory systems, but this is not to say there are only seven systems. There are ongoing discussions into precisely how many senses we have; these are explored a little below, but they are worth looking into further if you are curious about the sensory world.

Were I to choose an eighth sense, I would be likely to plump for the somatosensory sense. The somatosensory system has receptors all over the body. Those in the nose can be triggered by strong odours, meaning a strong smell can cause pain or sensations of hotness or coldness. Being aware that smell can cause pain and that people who are otherwise unable to smell may be able to register some scents through this eighth sensory system can come in handy when engaging Sensory Beings with olfactory experiences.

Types of smells likely to be picked up by the somatosensory system are those 'hot' smells, like chilli, pepper, cinnamon and so on.

Experience is personal

All experience is personal to the individual: we cannot state with any deserved confidence that "this is what is happening"; we can only state "this is what is happening for me in this context." When we work to support someone occupying the sensory world, we need to pay primary attention to *their* responses so that we can try and get a sense of what is happening for *them*, not what we *think* we are causing to happen. Deferring to our own experience and assuming that experience is the same for everyone is all too easy to do and is just as likely to lead us astray as in the right direction. That we enjoy a smell, or any other sensory experience, does not mean the person we are supporting will enjoy it. Smell is one to be especially cautious of because of its emotional content. To overwhelm with smell can be particularly distressing.

All the time we are working with the senses and a Sensory Being, we must be paying attention to how they are, and what responses they are giving; we are detectives trying to work out what their experience of the world is at that moment. Let the person you support be your guide as you hunt for sensory experiences together.

Sensory complexity

We have five senses?
Seven senses?
Nine?
Eleven?
How far do we go?

How many senses do we have?

How many senses do we have? Everyone knows the generally accepted answer is five: sight, touch, hearing, taste and smell. This answer covers most situations that people are consciously aware of both for themselves and for people they work with. So how many senses do we have? The highest number is 33 but 21, 14 and 9 are also valid answers. These include senses like Proprioception (body position awareness), Nociception (pain) and Thermoception (heat). What these senses make clear is that touch is a sense that unfolded into more sensory meanings. When a person touches a light bulb with their eyes closed; this is a touch event but it can also be broken into proprioceptive, nociceptive and thermoceptive events. Depending on the sensory capacities and biases of a person, it is important to know that there are more detailed ways of describing sensory events.

Alistair Somerville: Sensory Design Consultant; Cognitive Accessibility Specialist; Founder of Acuity Design. www.sensoryux.com

Deciding on how many senses we have is a little bit like deciding on how many colours there are: it depends on where we draw the lines. By some counts we have 33 sets of neurons that control our senses, so arguably 33 senses? Ultimately, when supporting a Sensory Being, what is important is not a head-count of what senses they have but an awareness of what their experience of their senses might be. Being aware of some of the delicious complexity of our sensory systems can open our eyes to aspects of that sensory experience that might otherwise elude us.

Recently I read a fascinating neuroscience paper (Brozzoli et al. 2014)[1] in which the researchers suggest that evolution has developed a set of neurons entirely dedicated to the space around the hand. They call this space the peri-hand space, and the set of neurons they have identified in relation to it are *at a single-cell level*: touch, sound and sight neurons. The mind boggles. The brain is an amazing organ.

Brozzoli et al.'s research focuses on interdisciplinary findings about the processing of space near the hand, but from it we can glean some insights that might inform us as we work to support Sensory Beings.

Think about the space just around your hand: that is the space your hand occupies and about ten centimetres all around (for an adult, less for a smaller hand as the space is proportionate to the hand size). This is very important space: it is where you do stuff; things happen in this space. It makes sense that the brain would allocate extra resources to this space.

When you see something in the space around your hand, you use your visual neurons, just as you would when looking at something anywhere else. But because this something that you are looking at falls within your perihand space, when you look at it you can call upon not only your visual neurons, but also your perihand space neurons. In this way, you get a bit of 'extra' sensory perception in this space. So when we ask children to point at the words as they are learning to read, this is a good idea as we are giving them an extra set of neurons to try and decipher those little squiggles that make up the letters on the page.

The scientists researching the perihand space did tests on people with a specific brain injury. Understanding what someone with a specific brain injury can, or cannot, do tells us a lot about the functioning of the part of the brain which is injured in their case. Because the brain is such a complex organ, this type of research is a very fruitful field of study. In the research, the scientists carried out a simple test: they played a sound at a set volume whilst touching someone on their right hand. In one version of the experiment, the source of the sound was placed within the perihand space of the left hand, and in the other version of the experiment, it was placed outside of the perihand space on the left-hand side. In both versions of the experiment, the sound sounded the same to the ear. The only thing that varied between the experiments was the source location of the sound. In the experiment where the sound was played from outside of the perihand space, the subject reported being able to feel the touch on their hand and hear the sound. In the version of the experiment where the sound was played within the perihand space of the opposite hand, the subject could hear the sound but did not report being able to feel a touch on their hand.

The perihand space research is fascinating. Many Sensory Beings have complex impairments to their cognitive functioning. We do not know as we support them precisely which parts of their brains are working as a typically developing brain would and which parts are not. If parts of their brains are not working, the impact of this on their sensory perception will be similar to the impact of specific brain injury – meaning that the experiences of people with specific brain injury can give us insight into what might be going on for the person we support.

So what is happening? Why can the person in the experiment sometimes feel the touch to their hand and sometimes not? What does the sound they hear have to do with their tactile sensory system?

Sensory experiences can cancel each other out

For the person taking the test, one sensory experience is cancelling out the other. We know they are capable of processing both experiences, but under particular circumstances they are not capable of processing them both at the same time. I think this is an extremely interesting point for those of us who support Sensory Beings with complex brains to consider: processing capacity in the brain is limited, and these limits vary between brains. A brain limited in this way must make a choice when it receives sensory stimuli messages from the sensory systems between which to process and which to ignore.

Limited processing capacity is not something that is exclusive to people with brain injury or particularly complex brains; we all have a limit. Often mine is closer than I like to think. When I do things like stop walking so as to type a text message quicker, I am adjusting my behaviour to suit the processing speed of my own brain, and recognising that I have a finite processing capacity.

In terms of our practice, it is useful to be aware that it is possible that the person we support is unable to process the stimulus we offer because of other stimuli going on around them. We often chat away in a friendly manner as we support a person. It is worth questioning whether being silent might be a way of enabling someone to access more of the experience we are offering. What if our chatter knocks out their ability to process information from the sensory experience we offer? We cannot know for sure – all we can do is try different approaches and watch ever so closely for the responses.

Sensory experiences can heighten each other

Another interesting phenomenon the researchers discovered was that sensory experiences presented together could heighten experience. In a sense, this is the exact opposite of the cancelling-out result reported above. In this piece of research, they found that if a visual stimulus was presented to the left-hand side of the field of vision at the same time as a touch experience was presented to the left-hand side, people had heightened perception of the visual experience.

We can explore employing this capacity for sensory experiences to heighten one another as we share sensory experiences with the person we support. For example, we can move a light from the left of their vision to the right, whilst synchronously touching first their left arm and then their right. This is not to say performing such a move will necessarily heighten experience, only that it is possible that it could. Again, it is one to try and to watch closely for differences in response.

Take-away tips

- Smell is an emotional sense and has a strong influence over our bonding and connecting with others.

- Smells can be particularly comforting or distressing.

- Smell is a powerful connector to memories.

- The famous five senses that we learned at school are not the whole story; we have a great many sensory systems. If you are supporting someone who experiences impairments to one or more of their primary senses, finding out about the other, lesser-known senses can give you avenues into discovering experiences they will be able to engage with and enjoy.

- Sensory experiences can cancel each other out or heighten each other. When you are presenting a single experience to a Sensory Being, be aware of what other experiences there are around at the time and consider how these may be affecting the Sensory Being. Bear in mind that you are a part of the external stimuli; your actions have an impact on their experience, so if you are touching them, if you are chatting, think about using your touch, your words, as tools to heighten the experience. Avoid creating a background blur of sensations that mask the experience you are trying to offer.

Part B: olfactory experiences

In Part B, we look at how the olfactory experiences we have access to in early life can be used as a source of inspiration when looking for smells to engage Sensory Beings.

The development of smell

Most of our senses become active whilst we are still in the womb. A fetus begins to form nostrils from around seven weeks of gestation. By the end of the first trimester of pregnancy, most babies will have a little nose. Amniotic fluid passes through the nose and mouth and into the lungs as the baby's body gets ready for breathing, and sensing, after birth.

Amniotic fluid

We know that sensing is a two-part process, made up out of the retrieval of information from the world around us using our sense receptors and the interpretation of that information by our brain. A good starting point when thinking about the development of any sense is to think about what we first had the chance to practice this process with. The first smells a baby gets to practice its processing powers on are those of and in the amniotic fluid. Amniotic fluid smells sweet and carries any strong odours the mother ingests.

Sweet milk

Immediately after birth, most babies encounter breast milk or formula milk. Sweet milky smells are likely to be among the first processed by the brain. Personal experience also comes into play, so a baby born to a mother who sucked peppermints through her pregnancy to stave off morning sickness may have had quite a bit of practice responding to the smell of mint, whereas a baby born to a mother who craved spicy foods throughout pregnancy may respond positively to the corresponding spice smells.

A good place to start with smells for the person you support may be warmed sugary milk – warmed because this increases the volatility of the scent. Volatile here does not mean that you make the smell angry, but that heating the milk causes it to release more molecules into the air. It is these molecules that find their way into our noses and get picked up by our olfactory receptors.

Other very sweet smells may also be interesting, such as vanilla, over-ripe banana, hot fudge, honey on toast or fresh candy floss.

The early environment

Moving on from sweet warm milk, we can consider what other smells a newborn infant is likely to have had practice at smelling. Some of these will depend on the environment they began their life in. I grew up at sea, so my early smell-scapes were very different from those of friends who grew up on land. Once again, the difference in early life experience between those who received neonatal care and those who were able to go home from hospital directly after birth is significant.

Our own smells

More immediate than our environment is our bodies themselves and the smells they produce. Although you may not want vomit, sweat or excrement smells playing a role in the sensory experiences you are offering to someone, finding these smells disgusting is not automatic. We learn disgust. People who have not learned that poo is an unpleasant smell may quite enjoy it. Once again, you might not like the smell of poo, but this does not mean the person you support feels the same way. Indeed, many of the base notes used in perfume are made up of compounds similar to those found in poo. Try heavy molecular scents mentioned in the next section as an alternative to the scatological.

Poo smells!

It is possible to purchase faecal smells. During the writing of this book, I purchased a product called 'Liquid ass' which, rumour has it, was developed by the American military to help soldiers learn to recognise intestinal wounds on the battlefield. The truth of this is, I am sure, up for great debate; however, the plausibility of it smelling like a mixture of the contents of your lower intestine and exploded guts is less so. It was a very big nasal challenge for me, and I now insist people attending training days with me take it outside to experience it.

Take-away tips

- Sickly sweet smells are likely to appeal to Sensory Beings.

- Smells the body produces are often smells that people in the early stages of sensory development respond to. These may also be responded to by people losing their sensory abilities.

- Consider what environment the Sensory Being you are supporting experienced when they were very young; what would it have smelt like?

Part C: the olfactory process

Having an understanding of the physical process of smelling can help us to find and facilitate smell experiences that Sensory Beings can process and respond to. In Part C, we look at the process of smelling and the different types of scents our noses register. We also look at how we associate meaning and smell, and how important it is to actually go out and smell stuff when hunting for olfactory resources.

How we smell

The process of smelling involves dissolving scent molecules in our nasal passageways. It is important for us to be well hydrated as we sniff. When we support someone in accessing the sensory world, attending to what can first appear to be purely physical needs, such as the need for hydration, is an important part in our enabling them to engage.

Scents that we think of as 'lingering' can be easier for people who need longer amounts of processing time to engage with. Scents that quickly disperse may be gone before brains and sensory systems have got into sync. Excrement is one such lingering scent, but other scents with heavier molecules as base notes – such as rosemary, lavender and peppermint – are also long lasting. Using fresh herbs creates more natural scents to be enjoyed. If you tear them up a little, they will release more aroma. Try lemon balm, basil, mint, bay and fennel. Adding them to boiling water to make a scented potion can add to the impact of their scent, as the hotness lifts the scent molecules into the air quicker than if the herbs were cold.

Smell neurons

Inside our nasal passageways, we have ciliated neurons and microvillus neurons. Ciliated neurons collect information about the volatile scents and the microvillus neurons collect information about pheromone scents.

Pheromone scents

Pheromone scents that are likely to interest a Sensory Being are those that they have had most practice at smelling; these are likely to be the sweat smells of their nearest care givers or their earliest care givers. I understand that it is unlikely that you will want to go around harvesting other people's sweat. Similarly, I understand that harvesting your own sweat is unlikely to appeal (although I do expect some of the more adventurous ones among you to find a way – see the smell noodle in Figure 10.6.1). For these reasons, you may wish to look to other pheromone scents as substitutes. Musk-based essential oils and musk-based perfumes are made using the pheromone scents of other animals, scents from plants or synthetically generated pheromone scents, so these can be substitutes for human pheromone scents.

Volatile scents

Volatile scents that are likely to interest a Sensory Being are, again, those that are personal to them through their lived experience. If you do not know what these might be, look for particularly strong scents that are likely to send a bold message to the brain.

Identifying strong smells

When asked to name something with a strong smell, people often think of food. You may have a few ideas in your head right now: think about them – how many of them would you be able to sniff from a different room? Most of our ideas about food smelling come not from food having a particularly strong smell, but from food being something we hold an inch or so away from our nose as we shovel it into our mouths. Try putting other things that close to your nose, and you will discover they too have a lot to offer the sense of smell. When you are out hunting for smells, do not just look for food; pick everything up and get sniffing.

If you are trying to identify scents without literally going out and sniffing things, think about things that you have smelt when other people were interacting with them: perfumes, foods, flowers, etc.

Smell and meaning

We often have strong associations with smells; for example, fruity smells are thought to be cheering, zingy smells to be invigorating and gentler smells to be calming. It is likely that these associations come about through our cultural experience and interpretation, rather than being a fact in themselves. Although we are focusing on the experience of the person we are supporting, our personal experiences and associations count too. We are a part of the experience of sensory-being for the people we support, and how smells affect us will have a 'rub off' effect on them; so if smelling dewberry makes you feel young and vibrant whereas the smell of cherry reminds you of being ill, choose dewberry!

Impairments

Our different olfactory neurons are controlled by different genes. Complex genetic conditions or specific brain damage may affect the genes that control one set of olfactory neurons but not the other set. It is possible you could be supporting a person that cannot smell volatile scents, but can smell pheromones. Remember, even if you are supporting an anosmic – someone who has no sense of smell – they may still be able to respond physically to odours through their trigeminal nerve, part of the somatosensory system; try 'hot' smells such as cinnamon or chilli.

Chopping off your arms does not improve the functioning of your legs.

People sometimes believe that impairment in one sensory area leads to improvement in other areas; for example, people who are blind are often asked if they have an improved sense of smell. It is a common belief, but nonsense: akin to saying that if I chop off your arms, the functioning of your legs will improve.

Improvement in ability comes through practice. Although someone who loses a sense may well have cause to practice using their other senses more, the improvement of their other senses does not necessarily follow on from the loss.

Some mental health difficulties have been shown to impact our ability to smell.[2] In recent times, the government of the UK has been championing the idea of parity of esteem between mental and physical health, the implication being that these two *separate* aspects of health should be held in equal regard. I believe that in the future we will have a better understanding of just how inter-linked and interwoven these two strands of our being are. That our emotional state has an impact on a physical ability is one hint towards that interconnect-edness. Happily, engagement with the sensory world can help support mental and physical well-being for all of us Sensory and Linguistic Beings alike.

A meta language for smell

In the section above, I categorised smells as being fruity, zingy or gentle. I could add to these categories synthetic, natural, floral, herbal, spicy and so on. Although you probably have an idea of what I mean by all of these terms, there is no set frame of reference for us all to use. From time to time, people attempt to define our primary smells like our primary colours, but we have yet to col-lectively agree on what they are.

We are so sight-dominated that we measure out our experience of sight with increasing precision. Young children learn to identify the primary colours – red, yellow and blue – and move on to the secondary colours of green, orange and purple. As adults, we get ourselves into conversations debating the subtlest of colour differentials. I have an ongoing argument with a friend about whether a particular bag is blue or green (for the record: it is blue). Recently, I had an extended conversation with my sister debating the precise shade of grey with which she and her husband should redecorate their apartment. Conversations about smell seem so blunt in comparison: I once worked in a slum on the out-skirts of Nairobi, and I heard my fellow workers remark on the smell of open sewers as awful. If someone is wearing a nice perfume, or if a flower I pass has a particularly pleasant scent, I might remark on their niceness, but that is it.

Actually, if I think about my conversations about smell, a lot of them are about not being able to identify a smell: "Can you smell that?" "What is that smell?" "What is it that is making that smell?" "Where is that smell coming from?" I am fumbling about in the world of smell a virtual novice compared to my abilities to discuss the visual world.

Pushing ourselves to try to become more scent literate benefits our own engagement and enjoyment of life as well as our abilities to source interesting sensory experiences for the people that we support. Try smell walking (see box below) as an exercise to boost your olfactory literacy.

Get up and go

As well as this tendency to olfactory illiteracy, you may also find yourself hampered, as you search for smells, by another quirk of this fascinating sense.

Searching for smells is really something you have to actively do. I mean, you have to get up, go out and get smelling.

We do not have the same capacity to re-experience smells as we do for the senses processed by our thalamus. If you have heard a song, you can 'hear' it in your head again; you can even get it stuck there playing around and around as a musical earworm. If you have seen a picture, you can conjure up an image in your mind's eye. But if you have smelled a smell, you cannot have that 're-experience' feeling. You may hold onto some knowledge about it: you liked it, you did not like it, but you cannot bring it into your mind to weigh it up and make decisions about it.

It is possible you may be able to identify strong smells by remembering whether other people commented on being able to smell them also, or by remembering how far you were from the source of the smell when you were first able to smell it. But if you are looking for smells to be a focal point for sensory-being activities, my advice is to set aside some time, grab a bottle of water, and go out hunting for them.

Smell walking

Taking a smell walk can be a good way to get attuned to the power of smell and develop your awareness of the smells in your local area. Smell walking is an approach inspired by the work of Helen Keller, who developed tactile mapping. Smell researcher Kate McLean provides a 'Smellfie kit' guide to smell walking on her website: www.sensorymaps.com – I encourage you to have a go.

On page 12 of "Smellfiekit: A smellwalking guide" (http://sensorymaps.com/wp-content/uploads/2015/10/Smellwalk_Intro_Kit_%C2%A9KateMcLean_2015.pdf), Kate says:

> Smell remains an under-valued and under-researched sense which possesses the capacity to induce time-travel and momentary location-displacement, translating anonymous space into personalised place.

After you have tried smell walking, perhaps you could have a go at sound walking, beginning with listening to the sounds your own body is making and then moving outwards with an open ear to discover what you can really hear in the world around you.

McLean, K. (2013) PhD Abstract Version 3 (unpublished draft). PhD candidate at the Royal College of Art.

Take-away tips

- We have two types of smell receptors: ones for volatile scents and ones for pheromone scents.

- We need to be hydrated to smell effectively.

- Scents with heavy base notes can be easier to process and may be calming (e.g. lavender), whereas scents with a sharper tone can be invigorating and alerting (e.g. peppermint).

- Smell preferences are personal; the Sensory Being you support may love the smell of something you find disgusting.

- To identify smells, you have to smell things! Do not try to work out what makes for an interesting smell experience by thinking about it: hold things to your nose and sniff!

- The loss of one sense does not improve the functioning of the others. Practice improves function.

Notes

1   Brozzoli, C., Ehrsson, H. H. and Farnè, A. (2014) Multisensory representation of the space near the hand: From perception of action and interindividual interactions. *The Neuroscientist* Vol. 20, No. 2, Pg 122–135.
2   Bancroft (2010) available online at: www.newscientist.com/article/dn19305-depression-dulls-sense-of-smell/

Be aware that some essential oils can trigger seizure activity in people with epilepsy. What triggers a seizure for one person will not necessarily trigger a seizure for the next person. It is important when offering any new sensory activity to observe the person you are sharing it with closely and be aware of how they respond.

5

Stimuli for the auditory sense

Part A of this chapter presents the auditory experiences we respond to best as our hearing becomes attuned to the world. Part B suggests why we might want to seek out sounds that intermittently get responded to by Sensory Beings, as well as those that always yield a positive response. We explore different types of sound as we look for ideas for new sounds to share. We also look at swearing and silence as two very special types of auditory experience.

Part A: auditory experiences

Our early life experiences offer us a variety of gentle sounds, the experience of which is key to our developing the neural pathways required for processing auditory experience. Part A gives examples of these early sound experiences for you to use as inspiration as you create sounds for Sensory Beings to enjoy. We also consider how these sounds, from an education standpoint, can be viewed under many different curriculum headings.

In the womb

The first sounds we get to practice processing are the white-noise sounds from the swirling amniotic fluid in the womb and the steady beating of our mother's heart.

White noise

Many of us continue to find white-noise sounds comforting throughout life. People will remark on enjoying listening to the sound of the ocean breaking gently upon the shore, but it is likely that we find other white noises comforting without realising. The sound of an engine purring away in the background as you drift off to sleep can mean you fall asleep quicker than usual. Low-level white noise masks other small sounds which would otherwise trigger an 'alert' response in us, and in so doing contributes to a calming soundscape.

Heartbeat, literacy and cross-curricular studies

Rhythm plays a powerful role in music and also in the development of communication. Steady beats are likely to be interesting, engaging and comforting to people. Researchers have found that a person's ability to keep a beat is more predicative of their literacy skills than their mother's literacy levels.[1]

Literacy skills may not be something you naturally think of for the person you support, but just because someone is not going to be writing novels later in their life does not mean they do not benefit from developing their literacy. Think of literacy as being the skills involved in exchanging meaning. Early communication experiences count as literacy. Understanding rhythm and beat is an early communication experience, so being party to these sorts of experiences is being involved in literacy.

Expectation of the next beat in a sequence is one of the building blocks of an understanding of time and sequence. If we are viewing beat with an educationalist hat on, then when we keep a beat, we are doing literacy (exchanging meaning and expression), science (time) and mathematics (sequence) – all brilliant excuses to get with the beat.

Voices

Beyond the sound of white noise and the steady beating heart, during your early development, you probably heard a woman's voice and the voices of other family members as you floated around safe inside your mother's belly. If you can record the voices of those closest to the person you are supporting, these are likely to be sounds they enjoy responding to. If you cannot get recordings of the people known by the person you support, try finding female voices that might sound similar to those they are familiar with, and mix these with deep booming male voices for an interesting sensory contrast.

Beginning with sound

Begin with soft consonant sounds (e.g. M-mmm) and long vowel sounds (e.g. A-ahhh), these are often the first vocalisations people make and are great for tuning in to and responding to as their length allows for slower processing speeds. It can be fun to contrast them with harder, sharper consonant sounds, these can alert people to the activity that is going on even if they are not sounds they are able to latch onto and join in with.

Emmie Ward: freelance music and folk arts practitioner, Post Graduate Certificate (PGCERT) in Sounds of Intent, Co-Founder of Sound Tracks multisensory storytelling @SoundTracks16, Facebook: Soundtrackscollective

Motherese

Motherese is a universal nonsense language that parents naturally use with their offspring. In all languages, across all cultures, mothers (and fathers) use this sing-song language. Motherese is made up out of bits of the parent's actual language and associated nonsense syllables or words that fill in the gaps, creating the melody of the language.

A mother speaking a motherese based on the English language, upon observing her child fall over, might say: "whoopsie daisies, there we go, cuddley-wuddlely, doo-be-doe!" Although that looks ridiculous written down, try saying it aloud. If I had written "whoopsie daisies, there we go, doo-be, cuddely-wuddley," it would not sound right to you. You see: you already know how to speak motherese!

Many nursery rhymes are based on the rhythms and natural melodies of motherese. So what is it about these rhythms and melodies – why do we all use them? We use them because these are the sounds that children respond to best. The person you support will love these natural rhythms. You do not have to say 'babyish' things; you just have to create that natural sing-song melody of language. Try it. I warn you though: it is addictive. You may end up creating these rhymes all the time. Embrace it: it will keep your brain warmed up, and it unites us around the globe.

Singing

Singing is the natural next step from motherese. If you are a talented singer, or simply an enthusiastic one, find songs to sing with the person you support. Singing is a wonderfully bonding experience. Although the person you support may not be able to sing along with their voice, they will find their own way to join in with you in the song.

If you, like I, have no musical talent, it is worthwhile seeking out those people who do. Researchers found that people with profound disabilities were more likely to respond to talented musicians than to those of us who are just enthusiastic triers.[2]

Talk

Just because a person cannot talk themselves does not mean they do not enjoy being a part of conversation. Remember, conversation is turn taking, so say your piece and then wait as if listening to a reply. But it is not 'as if listening': you are going to fully listen. This means listening with all your senses and your instinct too.

Many Sensory Beings will join in with conversation in their own way. To listen to them, you have to learn to listen to the language they use. This may be a language of sound, but it could equally be a language of muscle movements, or subtle changes to their demeanor. Be respectful, and do not interrupt; wait until they have had their turn in your communication exchange before moving on to what you plan to say next.

This type of respect – waiting your turn, listening – is just as you would do with anyone else, but when chatting with a Sensory Being, you may have to do a little extra: you need to guard your conversation against intrusions from outside. Sometimes Linguistic Beings can assume that because they can talk, their conversation takes precedence over other communications. It is a bit like when someone answers their phone midway through a conversation with you. This hurts: your self-esteem is dented. How often must Sensory Beings have this experience: they were part way through a communication with someone when another person came in talking, and they lost the attention of their communication partner. It can send a strong message to those around you, and help to change the culture of a place, if you do not allow your communication exchanges with Sensory Beings to be trumped by conversations with Lingustic Beings.

Our own sounds: vocalisations

We have had a lot of opportunity to listen to and to process the sounds we create ourselves. Finding ways to give people the opportunity to listen to their own sounds can be a great way in to sensory-being. Sometimes this can be as simple as positioning someone in a location where their own sounds will be reflected back to them – or allowing them to pause in such a place and encouraging them to make sound – subway tunnels under roads are brilliant.

Simple gadgets, such as www.lakeshorelearning.com's 'Hear myself sound phone,' or even simpler resources, such as sound tubes – which are sections of flexible plastic pipe costing around a pound – are brilliant ways to enable people to hear their own vocalisations.

Create your own sound mantra meditation

This is an idea for shared time where there is a focus on experiencing quiet sounds and silence.

1   *Find a quiet space with minimal noise and interruption.*

2   *Experiment with sitting directly opposite or side by side with the person. Support them to sit as comfortably as possible.*

3   *Focus on breath by tuning in to their breathing patterns and echoing them with your own breathing. Make your breath loud enough for the other person to hear.*

4 Focus on sound by echoing sounds the person makes. If they make an agitated or stressed sound try to soften it, sing it and make a calmer sound when you reflect this back. If the person is not making any sounds you can introduce singing a sound such as a long vowel sound or an mmmmm.

5 Begin to discover a sound mantra collaboratively. The mantra could be a continuous sound or it could coordinate with the person's in breath or out breath. Find a rhythm that works. It is important to remember that hearing the silence in-between sound is as important as hearing the sounds.

6 Repeat the mantra together. Pay attention to any changes such as slowing down of breathing or stilling of movement that could indicate that the activity has been calming.

7 Create a cue to signal the end of the activity, such as holding the person's hands or touching their shoulder for a moment. Make sure whatever you do maintains a sense of calm and is not an abrupt ending to calm time together.

Emmie Ward: freelance music and folk arts practitioner, PGCERT in Sounds of Intent, Co-Founder of Sound Tracks multisensory storytelling @SoundTracks16, Facebook: Soundtrackscollective

Our own sounds: internal

Our bodies make a lot of noises: internal clicks, rumbles and gurgles. Our clothes make sounds as we move; fabric rustles against itself and our skin. We filter these sounds out so that we can focus on the ones in the world around us. This filtering of the sounds from within our own bodies is a learned skill. It is only through experience of hearing the world and hearing ourselves that we begin to discern which sounds are interesting to us, which sounds help us to connect with food, with safety, with community, and which do not. The person you support may still be deciding which sounds interest them most. There is no right or wrong answer to which sounds to attend to; each person will decide according to their life experience.

We need to be aware of what noises could be present in the environment for the person we are supporting. Our own experience is not a guide for the experience of others: what we hear is not necessarily what others hear. The sounds I think are pleasant and interesting are not necessarily those which you think are pleasant or interesting. The person you support may hear the sounds you offer to them through a cacophony of distracting bodily sounds; be aware that if their attention seems to be flickering in and out, there may be other sounds present that you are not aware of.

There are likely to be particular times of day when internal noises are more prevalent than others – for example, after feeding, or if a person is hungry.

Being aware that the person you support's soundscape is different from your own, and will be changing throughout the day, will lead you to experimenting with sounds at different times of day. You may find that a sound they do not respond to at one time will get a response at another time.

An environment for a natural orchestra

The natural internal orchestra provided by the body is not necessarily something to be combated. If these are the sounds the person you support enjoys, then, as well as trying to interest them in sounds that connect them with the external world, you may seek to allow them time to tune in to an internal concert now and again. Or if you listen closely, perhaps you could echo their internal sounds, using them as a stepping stone for inspiring interest in the external world.

Facilitating an experience of auditory sensory-being by allowing someone to tune into their body's sounds is to facilitate not by providing stimuli but by providing a facilitatory environment. Such an environment will be a quiet place where interruptions are unlikely. For example, a place with a lot of padding or soft furnishings will be freer from noise clutter than a place where furniture knocks together or creaks and wheelchair wheels squeak against hard flooring. Choosing a room away from any doors that are likely to be opened and closed nearby, or one that does not have a cupboard in it that anyone is likely to need to pop in to get something out of, is judicious.

It is easy to improvise little sound caves: throw a blanket over a tent (cut the bottom out of a pop-up tent to place it over a wheelchair); draw curtains around a bay window; drape a blanket over a table and place cushions beneath to lie on; hide in a clothes cupboard or open wardrobe doors and sit facing into the fabric shielded by the doors. Be aware of the safety of the person you support as you create these environments; make sure there is plenty of air flow through the space. Be aware also of how a person responds in the newly created environment; is it a place where they feel happy or anxious? Sometimes a person may need time to get used to a new environment. Simply creating it and placing them in it can be a bit of a shock. Building it around them, or building up the time you spend inside, are ways of gradually introducing new spaces.

Anechoic chambers, anxiety and difference

Anechoic chambers are extreme examples of the sorts of environments we have been discussing. These are specially constructed quiet rooms that have lots of fancy shaped padding on the walls and floor to prevent sound being reflected back at the person inside. Many people entering anechoic chambers report feeling anxious.

We are used to being in a particular soundscape. Entering another one triggers a stress response in the body because it is different; we do not know yet whether it is dangerous or not. The people reporting these stress responses are highly intelligent, able people. It is important that we recognise that feeling anxious in response to differing environments is not a flaw brought about by disability but something innate in us all.

Inside an anechoic chamber, people's awareness of the sounds their own body produces is heightened. People report hearing the fluids in their mouth, the blood pulsing through their brain, the noises their joints make, their breathing, the gurgling of their digestion. Some people report feeling as if they are being driven crazy by these noises; others enjoy the new insight into their own bodies. Some people find the quietness of an anechoic chamber so distressing that their brains create auditory hallucinations to comfort them; others enjoy the peace. Each person's response to sound and space is unique – totally dependent on the individual. This is as true for typically developing people as it is for those whose development is more idiosyncratic. The differing responses of people experiencing anechoic chambers stand as pertinent reminders of how our own experience is not a guide to the experience of others. We feel and experience life differently, whether we are disabled or not.

The everyday reverberations of sound off the objects in the environment around us tell us about the space we are in and help us to balance in that space. This accounts for why some people feel claustrophobic or dizzy and nauseous in anechoic chambers. These sensations are alarming; it is hard to concentrate and focus if you feel claustrophobic or like the world is spinning. For someone processing sound in a different way to us, these sensations could come about in environments with low reverb – for example, places with a lot of soft furnishings and drapery. Understanding that distress can be caused by the sensory environment helps us to be sympathetic to the experience of others, and gives us a starting point for finding ways to help those in distress – for example, by finding a different sort of environment.

Take-away tips

- Sounds heard from within the womb – white noise, heartbeat, particular voices – are likely to be easy for Sensory Beings to respond to and also to be comforting.

- It is natural to respond with anxiety to unfamiliar sounds and soundscapes.

Part B: auditory experiences to seek out

In Part A, we looked at the sounds we first encounter and considered why these might be a rich hunting ground for auditory stimuli to offer Sensory Beings. In Part B, we are going to look at some of the different types of sound the world has to offer and why exploring these might be fruitful. At the end of Part B, we look at two unique auditory experiences, swearing and silence, and unravel the merits of both.

Adventure into new sensory worlds together

It is tempting, when hunting for stimulating sensory resources, to just opt for things that always get a response. Resources that people consistently respond to are an easy way for us to feel we have been successful in our attempts to engage a Sensory Being with the sensory world. Of course, a consistent positive response is great, but it may actually be more exciting to find the sorts of experiences that sometimes get a response and sometimes do not, and work with these instead.

Why?

Because the sounds that always get a response are the ones that the ears know how to hear and the brain knows how to process. They are the sounds for which the wiring is already connected. For the sounds (and any other sensory experiences, for that matter) that sometimes get a response and sometimes do not, the wiring may be on the cusp of becoming secure. Working with these sounds will give the person you support extra opportunities to focus on them and process them, and through this repeated experience, that wiring could become fully established. Working with these sounds could ultimately give the person you support new sounds they are able to hear in the world. You would be extending the reach of their sensory world, making life that little bit bigger for them, which is why it is wonderful to go adventuring into new sensory realms together.

Types of sound

Different types of sound are processed by different places in the brain. It may be that the person you support is better able to process certain types of sound over others. Their brain may process different sounds at different intensities: they may find some sounds overwhelming, whilst other sounds are hard to register.

Consider different sorts of sound as you explore auditory stimuli with the person you support. Notice the responses and reactions of the person you support as you share sounds and build up a picture of what they like. (Notice how sight-dominated our language is: let us call it a tune instead: build up a tune of what they like!)

We have already discussed internal sounds, speech sounds, vocalisations and white-noise sounds.

Consider also the following.

Sounds that change pitch

The changing of pitch is something particularly interesting to the ear. We use it to alert people to danger, or to a need to respond. Sirens are a classic example. Swanee whistles are a simple way of creating a sound that changes pitch, or if you are feeling ambitious, you could try yodeling.

Short sounds

Crashes, bangs, pops, blips and beeps. Short sounds can wake us up, surprise us. Short sounds send adrenalin pumping through our veins and can lead to periods of heightened alertness. This kind of response could be useful if you are looking to get a reaction from a person, but you have to remember that this extra attentiveness does not come for free. Once adrenalin leaves our system, we are tired, and so a sound that initially heightens awareness could subsequently dampen awareness.

Crashes and smashes can often be quite funny too, which leads us on to the next type of sound.

Laughter

Laughter is a super sound. If you are fooling around and making yourself and others giggle as you support someone, that is a wonderful thing. Laughter is infectious, and your fit of the giggles can inspire a reaction in another person. Laughter is good for your mental well-being and the mental well-being of those around you.

Laughter

Laughter has enormous potential for enriching the lives of Sensory Beings, and the lives of those who support them. Laughter does not have to be spontaneous, you can force laughter. Forced laughter can release the same endorphins and has the same tension dispelling properties as laughter that begins spontaneously.

Moody moods get studied a lot but positive moods are beginning to receive more attention, studies are substantiating the benefits of laughter reported by people. Here are a few examples:

- *Laughter is a natural painkiller (Norman Cousins while suffering from chronic pain used laughter to ease his pain claiming that 20 minutes of laughter would give him two hours of pain free sleep 'Anatomy of an illness' is his book.)*

- *Laughter encourages us to be more present; it is a great way of being with a person in the moment.*

- *We learn to laugh before we learn to talk; through laughing we communicate, bond and connect with others.*

- *Laughter is contagious. Once you start it's hard to stop! This means that a forced laugh can generate a natural laugh and the benefits of this laughter can be enjoyed with those near you.*

If you want to try a little laughter here's a starting exercise:

- *Take a deep breath in, and on the exhale let out a little chuckle.*

- *Repeat, allowing yourself to relax more and chuckle a little louder.*

- *Do this a few times and you will begin to feel the endorphins flow around your body.*

- *If you feel comfortable keep going until you are fully laughing.*

- *If you do not feel comfortable do not worry, just practice and it will come.*

Katie Rose White: Certified Laughter Facilitator, Founder of The Best Medicine, https://thebestmedicine.co.uk

Clear sounds

Pure notes, rounded, ringing out, clear sounds are especially beautiful to the ear, and often associated with times of wonder. Singing bowls, metal chimes, the notes from a flute, all fall into this category.

Long, deep sounds

Long, rumbly, resonant sounds are great for getting responses. Their duration means people have time to tune into them. Bear in mind, for some individuals it takes minutes, not seconds, to tune into a stimulus. Something like a didgeridoo playing could be just the ticket. Deep sounds that reverberate can be felt throughout the body, so a person will have other sensory systems they can call upon to let them know a sound is happening.

Jangly sounds

Jangly sounds are often easy to pick out against a noisy background. Things like bells, keys, cutlery and coins are all easy to make jangly noises with.

Sounds of Intent

The Sounds of Intent project is a joint initiative of the University of Roehampton, the UCL [University College London] Institute of Education, and the Royal National Institute of Blind People (RNIB). The project helps practitioners understand the musical development of children and young people with learning difficulties, from those who are functioning at a sensory level to those with advanced skills who are on the autism spectrum. Sounds of Intent provides suggestions for activities and enables practitioners and parents to record the achievements of their children. The Sounds of Intent resources are freely available at www.soundsofintent.org.

Music is a wonderful tool for engaging with those who understand and respond to the world in sensory terms: nothing offers a richer auditory experience, and nowhere else are the qualities of sound organised with such precision and mapped out with such perceptual clarity than with music.

Sounds with different qualities can be structured in different ways, resulting in differing musical styles and genres. Each genre offers a distinct type of auditory experience. It is wonderful for those in the early stages of musical development to have the opportunity to experience a wide range of pieces in different contexts. Think of the possibilities: from ragtime to reggae, folksongs to fugues, symphonies to spirituals. And there are just as many possibilities when we think of the variety of instruments available to explore: from drum kits to didgeridoos, gamelans to electric guitars and so on. There are high-energy pieces with loud, rapidly-changing streams of sound (try house music) and quiet, reflective works that present slow-moving auditory landscapes (try the Gregorian chants of monks).

Familiarity is important for all of us, and for those who process sound and music in a purely sensory way, high levels of repetition in order for them to be able to connect with what they are hearing. We advise you take an imaginative, flexible approach, but couple it with systematic observation so that you are as informed as you can be about how the music is being received. Above all, it should be fun!

Adam Ockelford: PhD, Associate of the Royal Academy of Music (ARAM), Professor of Music at Roehampton University. www.soundsofintent.org

Being babyish or respectful

Sometimes people are worried about sensory engagement work being 'babyish.' I have had conversations with people who support Sensory Beings in adult care who want to do sensory engagement work but are worried about being disrespectful of age.

Of course, some sensory experiences may appear babyish to the outside observer as they will use items similar to baby toys, or even baby toys themselves. But sensory experiences do not *have* to be babyish. Sensory experiences are not restricted to infanthood. We continue to have and seek out sensory experiences throughout our lives. Providing interesting sensory experiences that are not babyish is simply a matter of evaluating the experiences you meet in life and sourcing really good ones.

If you only hunt for sensory experiences in children's shops or in baby sections, then of course you will go home with things that people associate with early childhood. But shop in a DIY store or local supermarket and you will come home with different items that are just as sensory. Personally, I now travel around with a tattoo gun in my box of tricks: a real one, adapted for me by a very kind tattooist. It is very sensory (loud, vibrations, light, touch) and it is certainly not babyish. Another auditory experience that has particular sensory strength and is certainly not babyish is swearing. . . .

Swearing!

Of course, swearing at a person is just as disrespectful, if not more so, than offering babyish experiences. But there are ways to go about swearing that are not disrespectful, and actually 'not swearing' could be viewed as treating someone as less than equal and so be equally as disrespectful as being patronising.

Swearing is sensory

The amygdala is involved in the processing of swear words, but not in the processing of everyday language. The amygdala is part of the limbic system in the brain, strongly connected to emotion and memory. We tend to be introduced to swear words in highly emotive moments, making them particularly memorable and easy to learn.

There have been instances of people who have sustained a specific brain injury to the language processing centers of their brain who have been unable to speak, but still able to swear. People with aphasia often retain the ability to swear but find other language tricky; this is also true for aphasiacs whose first language is sign language. The right hemisphere of the brain is able to process swear words as a motor function, whereas we rely on the left hemisphere of our brain to process words as a language function. Swearing and processing swear words is physically different to the production and processing of everyday language, meaning that swear words hold a special sensory power.

Clearly, swearing is vulgar, disrespectful and undesirable in terms of a polite society and correct etiquette. But that is one side of the coin; on the other side, researchers[3] found a correlation between the number of swear words a person used and their vocabulary and intelligence. A correlation is a weak measure; however, that these two things correlate in a way that is contrary to what we are told as teenagers – that swearing is an indication of a limited vocabulary and low intelligence – makes this particular correlation interesting. The researchers found those who swore the most tended to be those with larger vocabularies and greater intelligences.

Researchers[4] found that swearing helps us to cope with difficult situations: just the type of situations that inspire it. Subjects exposed to pain and allowed to swear in response to it were able to withstand the pain for longer than those asked to bite their tongues.

Of course, swearing can be wrong and disrespectful; but we all know swear words, and from time to time they get used. If you are worried about disrespecting someone by being 'babyish,' consider that treating them as a special case, treating them differently to how you would treat a peer, is also disrespectful. If you are a person who swears, perhaps the person you support would enjoy being included in your bad behaviour.[5]

There are ways to go about exploring swearing that are appropriate and ways that are not. I am not in any way suggesting you should swear at a person aggressively; such a notion is so abhorrent, there should be no need to state it. Possible appropriate avenues to swearing include plays and poems that include swearing, theatrical performances that employ swear words, and comedians who swear for comic effect. In all of these situations, swearing is something that we are exposed to voluntarily. Those offended by swear words can choose not to attend or listen; those who enjoy colourful language are free to take part.

Finding ways to give the person you support the opportunity to take mischievous pleasure in swearing is respectful of them as autonomous beings.

Joyful swearing

Keith Park has been a leading light in the world of interactive Multisensory story for more decades than he cares to remember. He is enthusiastic about joyful swearing and recommends 16th century cursing as an entertaining route into vulgarity. Here he shares a few of his favourite cusses and gives a little advice as to how to go about using them. These are all from Shakespeare, mainly Henry IV, parts 1 and 2:

Flesh-monger!
Scullion!
Rampallian!
Lily-livered boy! (in the context of the 16th century, this is very nasty)
Clay-brained guts!
Bolting-hutch of beastliness!
You eel-skin!

Caitiff!
Thou art like a toad!
And two of my favourites:
You fustilarian, I'll tickle your catastrophe! (Henry IV, part 2)
and
Thou whoreson zed! Thou unnecessary letter! (King Lear)

Try shouting them out very loud, in a mock-angry voice, with lots of contempt, while staring at a colleague or friend in a nasty threatening way and stamping your feet. 'You eel skin' is especially wonderful!

Keith Park: International Inclusive Interactive Storytelling Specialist, Teacher, Author, and general mischief maker. @Keithpark1Park

Silence

Finally, silence: the most inclusive of sounds and often the most elusive. When we work with sound, often we are seeking to elicit sound from a person, either from their voice or from an instrument. We are pressured to create sound, to contribute to conversations, to be heard, to join in. Being allowed to not make sound, being given the opportunity to listen, to be in silence, is wonderful. And it is also active; this is why I call it the most inclusive of sounds, because for it to exist, everyone present has to contribute. A violinist can create a note on their own, a singer can sing whether others join in or not, but silence is always collaborative.

Silence is rare in the modern world, even feared. People worry that without sound as a distraction, unwanted thoughts will overwhelm them. People carry sound around with them, fearing boredom without its presence. People often seek to serve others by providing them with sound: switching the TV or radio on, or chattering. But silence might not be the monster we suspect it of being. Silence can be gentle and restorative. Silence can be a chance to notice other things, to communicate in other ways. Silence is also a chance to listen.

Sharing a silence with another person can be particularly precious as you both agree to be in each other's presence without the reassurance of sound. You are both gifted the presence of another person who asks for nothing in return; they are willing to just be with you whether you say anything or not. Silence is very accepting. Perhaps moments of silence will be a type of sensory-being that the Sensory Being you support finds nourishing and restorative.

Silence

Silence is where trust can grow. It deepens whatever connection was there in the first place. I keep a treasure chest of silences in my memory. Here are three silences from my life experience that are precious to me:

Minding my first grandchild when he was just a week old. Lying on the bed with him on my chest. No reading. No radio. Just this tiny person and me. Silent communication of total trust.

In the midst of the turmoil of puberty it was my turn to do the dishes with my father. This had always been awkward because I did not know how to speak to him, but one time he said, "Tell me, what shall we be silent about today?" which made me feel much better.

This last I found in my mother's diary from 1945. Her father, my grandfather, is sick and she enters the room to find him reading silently to himself. I am three years old and sitting on his bedside. My mother is amazed by the silence and asks me what I am doing there. "Listening to Grandad" was my reply.

In my life as a Quaker I regularly find communion in creating silences with other people. I hope these treasures of silence I have shared with you remind you of the deep connection silence can foster.

Ute Caspers: Peace activist; Peace envoy to South Africa and Israel and Palestine; instrumental in introducing Alternatives to Violence projects in Germany and South Korea; trainer in non-violent conflict resolution; Backhouse lecturer 2004; volunteer hospice worker; Quaker; very cherished Grandmother and honorary Grandmother.

Take-away tips

- Giving Sensory Beings the opportunity to practice responding to new stimuli can ultimately increase their ability to perceive and engage with the world, so do not just stick to the experiences they already know and respond to.

- Different sounds are processed in different areas of the brain, so sensory sensitivities to sounds may be different for different types of sound.

- Swearing is sensory and can be good for you!

- Pauses and silence are an important part of experiences of sound and of communication.

Notes

1   Nina Kraus is a good researcher to look up if you are interested in learning more: www.brainvolts.northwestern.edu/

2   Wylie, A. (2015) Soundbath: An innovative approach to music with children. *PMLD Link* Vol. 27, No. 2, Issue 81, Pg 26–29. www.pmldlink.org.uk/wp-content/uploads/2015/09/PMLD-Link-Issue-81.pdf

3   This article references many papers relevant to the topic of swearing: Jay, T. and Janschewitz, K. (2012) The science of swearing. *Observer* (Association for Psychological Science), May/June. www.psychologicalscience.org/index.php/publications/observer/2012/may-june-12/the-science-of-swearing.html

4   Stephens, R., Atkins, J. and Kingston, A. (2009) Swearing as a response to pain. *Neuro Report* Vol. 20, Issue 12, Pg 1056–1069.

5   It is judicious to seek consent from family and carers if you are considering using swearing with an individual.

6

Stimuli for the gustatory sense

In the first part of this chapter, we look at the mechanics of taste and consider how gustatory experience is not all about the tongue or eating. Part B takes you through the taste experiences likely to appeal to Sensory Beings, and Part C looks at the influence of how food behaves in the mouth on our gustatory experience. We consider how we each experience taste differently and look at how to go about introducing eating to a Sensory Being.

Part A: how we taste: it is not all about eating

Here we examine the mechanics of gustatory experience. Taste is not all about the tongue; other sensory systems inform what we think of as our experience of taste. Similarly, taste is not all about eating, so we also examine how you might safely go about facilitating gustatory experiences for someone who is not able to eat.

The mechanics of taste

Our tongue has thousands of taste buds which renew themselves throughout our lives, changing as they do so. In our early development, they are particularly good at picking up sweet and salty tastes. Later in life, this sensitivity deteriorates, meaning as we age, we can cope better with foods and drinks we would have previously found unpleasant.

Our taste buds play a role in helping us to moderate what we eat; for example, we need a bit of salt in our diet, so our initial response to salty foods can be one of great delight, but if we eat too much, our taste buds will begin telling us it tastes horrid.

A misunderstanding about there being different zones on the tongue for registering different flavours stood for years in the scientific community before being widely debunked. The debunking of this idea is easy to do yourself with a cotton bud and some different flavours. Dab a flavour onto different areas of your tongue. You will find you can taste each flavour all over your tongue.

Taste is not all about the tongue

Our tongue, for all its fabulousness, is actually a pretty basic sense organ registering the five basic tastes: sweet, sour, salty, bitter and umami (a savoury taste associated with monosodium glutamate). It is only when our nose gets involved that we begin to experience the range of flavours we know and love, or loath. To prove this to yourself, you need a flavoured sweet. I like to use jelly beans with different flavours. What you are going to do is retro-nasally taste the jelly bean, which in itself is a wonderful phrase. Hold your nose clamped shut with your fingers, place the jelly bean in your mouth and begin to chew. What you will experience is a generic sweetness: this is the sweet that your tongue can register when it works alone. Now let go of your nose; suddenly, you will be hit with the flavour of lemon, or cola, or cherry, or whatever the jelly bean's flavour is, demonstrating what a big role your nose plays in your experience of flavour. Try this in a room with a lot of people and you will also get a very satisfying 'ooo' sound.

As well as being fun, retro-nasally tasting sweets highlights something important when we are considering offering taste experience to Sensory Beings. To be able to access taste experiences in all their glory, the person you support will need to have their nose working, as well as their mouth and tongue. Someone hooked up to an oxygen supply may not get the same smell experience of food as someone without an oxygen supply. Someone with a damaged nose, a cold, or an allergy may not get the same smell experience of food as someone with a healthy nose. Similarly, our ability to smell can decline in later age, which will have a knock-on effect of making tasting things less interesting. Without being able to use your sense of smell in conjunction with your sense of taste, there are just five flavours; with it, there are millions.

Employing other sensory systems to support engagement with taste

Someone exploring eating without a good sense of smell backing up their experience may find it rather dull. We can add interest by thinking about the tactile and somatosensory[1] potential in food, i.e. by trying to create meals with different textures and temperatures so that there is something to interest and engage the senses beyond flavour.

Taste is not about eating

Taste is not a sense reserved for exploration by those who can, or who may one day, eat. Exploring taste exercises the muscles in the mouth, which are useful for sound making and breathing, as well as for eating, so exercising these muscles is very beneficial even before you begin to take into account the life-enriching properties of stimulating another sense.

People who have a gastronomy tube, allowing them to be fed directly into their stomach, may still experience the taste of the foods pumped through the tube when they burp. Knowing what these foods taste like is a useful piece of information for you as you explore taste experiences to offer them. What these foods taste like is also a relevant consideration for someone who was previously fed via gastrostomy but who is now able to eat orally, as they will form part of their early experiences of taste.

Eating experiences

Food is a huge source of pleasure in life, and sharing food is a fundamental part of all cultures; imagine not being able to take part. You might not be allowed food, because you can't swallow safely. Maybe you have a nose or stomach tube. Perhaps your sensory issues are so extreme that you can't even tolerate the thought of eating. Then think what it must be like if you can't tell anyone how it feels.

I've been giving people with feeding difficulties the sensory pleasure of eating, even if they're unable to eat normally. I use facial massage to help Bob feel what it's like to properly close his lips so that he can swallow his saliva. I use chewy tubes to give Sarah the sensory experience of chewing, strengthening her jaw and tongue muscles so that she is less likely to gag on lumpy food. Philip uses bite blocks to help with his jaw movements so he knows how much to open his mouth for a spoonful of yoghurt versus a sandwich. Amelia enjoys playing with strong smelling foods. These people deserve to experience the joys of food.

Mags Kirk: BSc (Hons), Independent Speech and Language Therapist at Two Can Talk. www.tctspeechtherapy.co.uk

Taste safely

Not everyone can safely explore taste. If you are at all concerned about the safety of taste experiences for the person you support (as with any sensory experience), consult with the relevant medical professionals first. Assuming the person you support has the capacity to explore taste and it is medically safe for them to do so (be aware that tasting stimulates the production of saliva, so those not able to swallow may need support with suctioning to safely have these experiences), where do you start?

Take-away tips

- Taste is a sense you should look to engage for all Sensory Beings, including those who are unable to eat orally.

- Taste is a relatively weak sense on its own, but when working in partnership with smell, through it we can access a multitude of flavours.

- Other sensory systems can be utilised to support a person in accessing taste experiences.

Part B: gustatory experiences

In Part B, we look at gustatory experiences likely to be good starting points for exploration of taste and where they might lead on to. We also consider the influence of differing life experiences on the sorts of flavours likely to yield a positive response from a Sensory Being.

Begin sweetly . . .

Start to explore taste with sweetness. We have all practiced tasting sweetness in the womb. The taste of amniotic fluid, which is swallowed by the fetus from around 12 weeks of gestation, changes, but is often sweet.

The taste of amniotic fluid can also sometimes be salty or bitter. Researchers have been able to identify, later in fetal development, facial expression responses made by the developing child to the taste of the amniotic fluids, and also behavioural responses with fetuses stopping drinking when the fluids taste bitter. Regardless of culture and race, we are all born with a sweet tooth, and in general we all keep it as our body drives us to seek out the energy associated with foods that taste sweet.

. . . and branch out.

Once you have begun exploring taste experiences with the person you support, you can branch out and try some more adventurous oral experiences – for example, sherbet, which still has sweetness but accompanies it with an acidic kick. Salty is often the next favourite flavour we enjoy as we develop. Salty foods can be interesting taste experiences to explore as they often occur in conjunction with the tactile experience of crunchiness. Crunchiness signals freshness and therefore safety to our brain, which means we are likely to prefer foods with a bit of bite to them than mushy ones.

Bitter taste experiences such as coffee, which many proclaim to delight in, are always learned. We have to forcibly teach ourselves to enjoy them, and pleasure in them takes quite an act of will as we repeatedly expose ourselves to the flavours and practice our responses. Personally, I have found major life events, such as relationship changes and motherhood, to be a powerful spur to pursuing an interest in coffee.

Early taste experiences

The tastes of our childhood and early experiences of life are likely to be ones we continue to respond to positively throughout life. Think about what these early taste experiences would have been for the Sensory Being you are supporting. You are not looking to identify the extraordinary special treat foods that they might have encountered on special occasions (although these are good to know about too); you are more interested in what the everyday food would have been in their early life. Did they eat lots of porridge? Lots of rice and peas? Was spaghetti on the menu every day of the week?

Take-away tips

- We all have a sweet tooth, and none of us naturally like bitter flavours; we have to drill ourselves to respond positively to them.

- Find out what the Sensory Being you support ate as a child and try some of these flavours, textures and smells with them now.

Part C: how food behaves

In Part C, we explore how different physical properties of food alter our gustatory experience. We recognise that our experience of flavour is individual, that what I might consider a pleasant taste may be unpleasant to you. And we note the importance of not putting someone under pressure to eat.

Sucking

If you are using food to explore taste, think about how it behaves in the mouth. Something like a gulp of orange juice swooshes over our sensory receptors and is gone in a moment. There is very little time to process the information. Sucking fluid through a straw slows its transit over the tongue, giving the brain more time to process the information it is receiving. Sucking has a bonus sensory effect as it stimulates the vestibular system. The muscles involved in sucking are also very useful in shaping word sounds and in holding the mouth closed when not in use, minimising dribbling.

Fatty

Fatty foods carry their flavour in the fat molecules. These take longer to dissolve on the tongue, dispersing more slowly than non-fatty foods. Chocolate is wonderful (for all the obvious reasons) and for its slow-release, sweet taste.

Hardness

Foods that provide resistance to the teeth and muscles of the mouth as they close around them send extra information to the brain about their presence in the mouth and so may be easier for an individual to notice and respond to.

Chewy

Chewy foods take longer to be processed than liquids or more tender foods. The length of time taken to process the food means that messages about the taste and flavours of the food get sent for a longer period to the brain, allowing the brain more time to respond to and begin to process these messages. Special pouches can be purchased to put food into which allow for food to be chewed but not swallowed. Often these pouches are designed for weaning babies; you would need to check what effect having teeth has on them, but they should still be safe to use under close supervision.

Surprising

In the modern world, we have lots of food surprises. These come in many shapes and forms. A food surprise could be a flavour that you have not had any experience of, perhaps something from a different cultural tradition. Try talking to friends from around the globe; ask them what food they would miss if they lived in a different country. Synthetic foods such as popping candy can provide big sensory surprises: exploding on the tongue, stimulating the tactile, somatosensory, gustatory, auditory and olfactory senses, all in one go.

Experience is different

The person you support may process taste in a different way to you. They may be hyper-sensitive to taste or hypo-sensitive, meaning they can only tolerate very weak flavours or will need a very strong flavour in order to be able to register the taste.

Differences in experience of taste are common to us all. We know from the taste responses of our friends that we all have different taste preferences.

However, for the person you support, these differing responses may be more pronounced, especially if they are someone who has a condition that affects their brain.

Start slowly, taste with your fingers

It is important to start slowly with taste and not put pressure on the person you support to engage with an experience. Remembering that smell is a part of tasting, you can explore food and drink with the hands and nose first. If this exploration leads to some food being tasted, then so much the better. Leave this discovery to happen naturally rather than force it. Often it will be a more interesting, engaging experience if it is one the individual has discovered themselves, rather than if they have been heavily cajoled to pick something up and taste it.

A sensory food toolkit

Sustainable design is about using design as a tool to improve lives. I was moved by the thought of some people leading lives without the experiences associated with eating.

For me one of the most engaging sensory experiences is food. I think of squeezing citrus fruit; hearing the flesh burst as you bite into it, the sweet bitter taste on the tongue and the rich aroma in the air. I was determined to find a way for Sensory Beings to engage with food.

In my research I asked Linguistic Beings about their favourite sensory experiences related to food, people talked of baking bread, melting chocolate and brewing coffee. Their eyes would light up in excitement demonstrating the power of food experiences in our lives. The Sensory Being Consultants we worked with on the Sensory-being project gave me great feedback on my early prototypes. They taught me the importance of creating something which can be interpreted in each individual's own way.

My aim was to create a sensory toolkit, a recipe as such, for facilitating the sensory experiences associated with food for Sensory Beings who cannot eat orally. The toolkit gives food related experiences through smelling, squeezing, seeing, and hearing. Taste is included of course, but the kit recognises that other senses play just as big a role in enjoying food and a person does not have to be able to taste to be able to share in the pleasure of food. I wanted the kit to encourage group activity as food is also a time for social interaction and sharing.

Arthur Holt: Sustainable design student Falmouth University, Passionate cook, ultimate Frisbee player and sea swimmer. You can find out more about Arthur's design in the online Chapter 10 on http://jo.element42.org/the-sensory-being-project

Take-away tips

- Think about how taste experiences are accessed physically (sucking, biting, crunching, chewing) and offer varied experiences to the Sensory Being you are supporting.

- Think about how different foods offer different processing experiences – for example, foods that send particularly bold messages, such as sherbet, and foods that allow for slow processing speeds, such as chocolate.

- Putting pressure on someone to eat is counterproductive in the long run.

Note

1   For information on the somatosensory system, see the section titled "Pain" in Chapter 4.

7

Stimuli for the tactile sense

Touch is a sense often used to attempt to engage Sensory Beings, but are we offering the scope of experience that we might, and are we understanding the responses to our approach accurately? In Part A of this chapter, we look at some of the counterintuitive notions when it comes to understanding tactile experience and people's responses to it. In Part B, we look at what sorts of touch experiences we might look to offer Sensory Beings as a stimulus for sensory-being.

Part A: understanding touch

Touch is a curious sense when looking for early responsive experiences for Sensory Beings, because our first instincts are not always right and the stimuli we are searching for can be quite counterintuitive. For example, most people approaching an individual with profound and multiple learning difficulties for the first time will offer the gentlest of touches. They do so out of a mix of respect and fear: they do not want to startle or hurt the individual before them, who they perceive as being incredibly fragile. People respond similarly to newborn babies, and to those in later age who also appear terribly fragile. The common instinct is for a gentle stroking touch, but if we are looking for the touch experience most likely to yield a positive response, this is not the one to go for. In fact, a gentle touch can cause some people pain.

In Part A, we look at the counterintuitivity of gentle touch, and learn how touch plays a critical role in our development and ongoing well-being. We look at how touch policies can be judiciously used to support positive touch practice. We also consider rejection and overload as two more responses to touch whose interpretation can be counterintuitive.

Gentle = painful

A Gentle Caress is a glass sculpture made out of triangles of orange, pink and yellow glass. It can be viewed on: http://clairehillglassart.co.uk/a-gentle-caress/. The sculpture represents what gentle touch feels like to Claire Hill. Claire writes:

> *I do not enjoy the sensation of having someone stroke my arm/back or legs. It feels like prickles all over my body and I become very angry quite quickly if someone does it. I have to work hard not to express displeasure in inappropriate ways e.g. lashing out or shouting.*
>
> *I really appreciate when people ask whether it is ok to touch me, or at least warn me beforehand that they are going to do it.*
>
> Claire Hill: Glass Artist. http://clairehillglassart.co.uk;
> Qualified Teacher Status: Former Special Educator. Proud Aspie.

Try it on yourself

Use a single finger to very slowly and gently touch the back of your hand, and think about how each step of this experience feels. Your first experience of the touch will be the warmth of your finger approaching; perhaps tiny hairs on the back of your hand then pick up the sensation of the finger nearing your skin. As it first touches your skin, just the surface of your skin registers the touch – it is a tingly sensation, almost electric. Then, as the touch lowers onto the skin, that tinglyness disperses and the feeling is softer and warm. Finally, as you apply pressure to the touch, the deeper tissues of your hand register the presence of your finger and you feel a more secure, firm touch.

Imagine what that first sensation of touch would feel like to you if your sense of touch was turned up. That tinglyness would be sharper, and the electric feel would be more of a shock. It would be alarming, and it would hurt; it would feel as if it expressed cruelty, not kindness, and you might respond aggressively.

Touch and development

Touch is of enormous importance in our development. In the early 1900s, people believed that to cuddle children could lead to them becoming spoiled, and parents were advised against it. Scientists questioned this belief through a number of experiments, including Harlow's controversial wire mother monkey experiments conducted at the University of Wisconsin–Madison in the 1930s.

In one version of the wire mother experiments, baby monkeys were offered the choice of a wire mother which gave out food (simply a wire tube with a feeding tube poking out of it) or a cloth mother (a similar wire tube, but this time swaddled in a furry cloth) with no food. One might expect that the baby monkeys driven by a desire to survive would choose the mother with food, but overwhelmingly they chose to cling to the cloth mother.

Understanding has progressed, and along the way we have continued to gain insight from other horribly cruel situations. When the Romanian orphanages were opened in the 1980s, we learned, this time from humans, not monkeys, how damaging an upbringing without physical contact and affection can be. Children brought up with only their basic nutrition needs met were developmentally impaired. Lots of children did not grow to the height that would have been expected of them. Many children suffered permanent brain damage due to the neglect they endured.

Practitioner insight

When I was training as a nurse, I had to spend about six weeks in the training school, followed by six to ten weeks on a 'ward.' The wards were individual buildings with similar residents housed together. One of my placements was on an all-female ward of elderly people with moderate to severe learning difficulties. One lady in particular tugged at my heart strings: she was 'hidden away' at the hospital because she 'bore a child out of wedlock' when she was 16 – she was 83 when I met her! She had spent 67 years in an institution for getting pregnant.

By the time I met her, she had lost her hearing and had very little vision, so communicating with her was difficult. When I read her notes, she was described as an 'idiot' and an 'imbecile' by the person who admitted her. However, she could read and write.

Unfortunately, years of institutional living had prevented her from practising and maintaining her skills, so all I saw was a sad, lonely lady who wandered around carrying a baby doll. I later discovered that her daughter, who had been born at the hospital, was also a resident on a different ward. There was no evidence that she had learning difficulties, and no evidence to suggest that they had spent any time together since she was a baby. Heartbreaking.

I wish I had known then what I know now. I would have tried so hard to help the mother connect with the world around her, and possibly have a relationship with her daughter. Physical touch between staff and residents was not exactly frowned upon, but definitely discouraged. When I was administering medication, or helping with meals, the mother would sometimes hold my hand. I allowed it for a few seconds, but conscious of the ethos, I would remove her hand from mine. If only I had the courage back then, when I was young, naïve and conscious of my peers' opinions, that I have now, I may have made a huge difference to an old lady's final years. What a missed opportunity.

Neonates

In recent times, we have begun to apply what we know about the importance of touch in medical settings. Babies born prematurely have high healthcare needs; often these are met by placing the babies in incubators and hooking them up to all sorts of supportive machinery. Not so long ago, we would have thought this to be the most important thing to do, and to risk taking them out of that gadgetry for something as fripperous as a cuddle would have seemed irresponsible. But with an increasing scientific understanding about the importance of touch – not just emotionally, but physically from a developmental point of view – this is now precisely what happens. Ever so carefully, tiny babies are lifted out of their incubators and unhooked from some of their tubes, whilst others are tentatively transported with them, to be placed against the warm and loving skin of a parent. They are touched, cuddled, held, stroked and massaged.

What is the impact of touch on neonates? In a review of the scientific literature in this area, Kulkarni et al. (2010)[1] report that neonates respond to this touch by showing increased weight gain; better sleep patterns; enhanced neuromotor development; stronger emotional bonding; and reduced nosocomial infection, which in turn led to reduced mortality rates. Other researchers have found touch helped babies cope with times of stress, and that the opportunity for contact has resulted in fewer babies being abandoned by their parents during these difficult times. What we would previously have thought of as just an emotional need is now being recognised for its very real benefits to physical health.

Touch is a part of health for us all

Mental health and physical health are not separate distinct entities, but two parts of the same whole. Whilst neonate studies offer an extreme example of this duality, we must remember touch is important for all. Some people live in situations where touch is limited for institutional reasons; for example, teachers going through teacher training are often told that it is inappropriate to touch students. This advice is given against a backdrop of fear of prosecution for inappropriate touch. And in a world rife with this fear, to be on the safe side, it is recommended that we do not touch at all. How sad. And how sad especially for Sensory Beings, for whom a nurturing touch may be one of the only ways they understand they are not alone in this world. Hopefully, in the future our understanding will have moved on and the advice will be to give appropriate touch and withhold inappropriate touch. In certain situations, it is inappropriate and indeed cruel *not* to touch.

Sensory Beings are particularly vulnerable to abuse; statistics show that individuals with learning disabilities or individuals in later age are more often victim to abuse than those who do not fall into these categories. Believing that preventing touch is preventative of abuse is naïve. Preventing touch dehumanises contact between people, alienating both parties from each other and contributing to an environment where abuse can thrive.

Touch policies

If you work within a setting where there are not clear guidelines on the use of touch, it may be wise to create some. A good starting point when writing a touch policy is to contact a setting similar to your own and ask for a copy of their touch policy. Touch should always be consensual. Part of your touch policy will address what consent looks like for the people you support. Consent can be a tricky topic, with Linguistic Beings being quick to assume it is something for which language is a necessary pre-requisite.

Whether you are writing a policy or simply interacting with a family member at home, I encourage you to pause and think about how the person you are sharing touch with communicates consent in the moment. If you know them well, you will know what they do when they like something and what they do when they do not like something. If you are just getting to know the person you are supporting, then you will be paying close attention to their responses and to your instincts. How do your interactions feel?

Another useful thing to include in a touch policy is a statement about what touch is used in your setting. People who feel nervous of using touch can equip themselves through the policy with a strengthening rationale for their actions.

An example of a statement of intent to touch from Newman School

www.newmanschool.co.uk

Newman School took inspiration from similar policies from Castle Hill School, Huddersfield, and Jack Tizard School, London in the creation of their policies and acknowledge the generosity of these settings in sharing their policies.

Statement of intent
Touch is used

- *to reinforce communication, for example, by placing a hand on the student's shoulder whilst speaking*

- *to give physical support and guidance*

- *to give reassurance: communicate security and comfort*

- *to physically intervene and manage behaviours (read in conjunction with our Positive Handling Policy)*

- *to play and interact*

- *to role model positive use of touch*

- *to respond non-verbally*

- *to direct or physically prompt*

- *to give personal care*

- *to give physical cues for participation or understanding*

- *medication/treatment – to offer support after seizure/injury*

- *to aid protection in hazardous situations*

- *to give therapy, for example: massage physiotherapy*

- *as the main form of communication*

- *to respond to students use of physical contact for communication and making social connections*

- *to reward and affirm*

- *to give the opportunity of choice to lead the communication*

- *to communicate warmth and a sense of mutuality, and enable the student to learn understanding of these things and the ability to communicate them*

- *to offer the opportunity to students who do not want or like touch to see the enjoyment and benefit of physical contact*

- *to give graphic experience of the tempo of life and physical activity enjoyed by another person, for example: a member of staff communicates calm and stillness through physical contact.*

- *Students with physical disabilities need support to touch and interact in ways that happen naturally with their peers.*

Intensive interaction

Dave Hewett, one of the early developers of intensive interaction, an approach to teaching the pre-speech fundamentals of communication to individuals with profound disabilities, wrote about the importance of touch in the *Support for Learning* journal: Hewett, D. (2007) Do touch: physical contact and people who have severe, profound and multiple learning difficulties. *Support for Learning* Vol. 22, No. 3, Pg 116–123.

The Intensive Interaction website: www.intensiveinteraction.co.uk has free downloads that may help you as you create a touch policy.

Rejection

Our first thought when someone rejects our touch, or rejects touching an object, should always be for their autonomy. Are they expressing a desire not to touch or be touched? Are we listening to and respecting their expression? If they do not want to be touched, they should not be touched. If they do not want to touch an object, they should not be forced to. Personal autonomy should always be respected; however, an initial rejection of touch experience does not always indicate a wish for the activity to cease.

The rejection of touch, whether human or of an object, is another place where the offering of tactile experience to a Sensory Being becomes curiously counterintuitive. It is relatively common for people to reject touch experiences: pushing them away, flinching from them, and so on. However, in a confusing world, where we must be detectives trying to understand the experience of another, rejection does not necessarily indicate that touch is unwanted.

John Ockenden, writing in the *PMLD Link* journal in 2006,[2] urges practitioners supporting people with profound and multiple learning difficulties to consider the response to a stimulus in one of three ways, not just the standard two of "yes" or "no." John's third option is an expression of "not yet" so that a response to an object can be interpreted as one of yes/no/not yet. In his article, John cites the inspiring work of McInnes and Treffry,[3] who in their study of deaf-blind children identified that rejection of an experience is the first and *expected* stage in a sequence of response to an opportunity.

Rejection is the first step to engagement

Let us be clear: the first step to engaging with a new opportunity is rejection. Initially this idea is counterintuitive, but with the application of a little thought and the concept of freedom, we can begin to make sense of it. None of us like to be forced to do an activity. Even if I were to choose your very favourite activity to force upon you, the very fact that I was forcing you to do it would cause you to resist. This is because, over and above the pleasure we take out of engaging with activities, we value our freedom.

If I were to suggest a new activity to you, this is what is likely to happen: you would feel a little hesitant at first, because you do not know if you will like this activity or not; then you would make a choice as to whether to take part or not, in the full knowledge that this choice is yours and that I am not going to force you to do whatever it is I am proposing. You are able to do this because of the way your mind understands the world: you know that your decision now affects a point of time in the future. You also know that an activity is time limited, i.e. it is not going to go on forever and ever; all these things and more feed into you being able to say "yes, I'd like to try that."

For Sensory Beings, their experience of the world is different: they do not have the option of drawing on all the different sources of knowledge you do. A Sensory Being must discover knowledge in the moment, and the absolute best way to find out if you are free to take part in an activity in the moment is to discover whether you can get out of it. Through repeated rejection, a Sensory Being discovers their freedom. As they push the tin of bells off the table for the hundredth time, they learn that this is an experience they can get rid of; and once they have learned that, they may begin to be willing to explore the experience – of course, stopping every once in a while to confirm that they can indeed be rid of it if they wish.

Rejection is a step on the path to engagement. So rejection does not necessarily mean the experience itself is rejected: as John Ockenden says, it is not a case of yes or no, but of yes/no or not yet. As we do our detective work, trying to understand the experiences of the person we support, it is our task to discern the difference between a "no" response, which equates to a refusal of consent and should mean we cease the activity and not repeat it, and a "not yet," which means we should withdraw the activity temporarily before offering it again later. There are no easy answers as to how to identify each response, as communication will be unique to the individual responding.

Rejection *can* indicate delight

Here is another twist to the intricacies of understanding this wonderfully counterintuitive world of touch. Research[4] into the responses of neonates to touch shows that if an experience is particularly attractive, this can lead to rejection. Once again, we can counter this counter-intuitiveness with the application of a little thought.

Neonates, like many Sensory Beings, are not in possession of fully regulated sensory systems. It is as if someone has a set of volume dials controlling the strength of the different sensory signals received by their brain and is playing around with them. A signal can be overwhelmingly strong in one moment and barely detectable in another. The metaphorical person twiddling with those controls is influenced by what the individual senses, so when something highly desired is sensed, all the controls get turned up really high to make sure the messages about the desired object get through. Sadly, this has the consequence of the messages coming through so strongly that they overwhelm. With their systems overloaded, a person must fight to get away from the object causing the overload or simply shut down and cease processing sensory information. Either way, they do not get to experience the item they so badly wanted to experience. This is made all the sadder if the person offering them this greatly desired experience only gives them one chance at accessing it, assuming from their rejection that it was not liked. By offering repeated opportunity for experience, we give them the chance of getting those dials under control so that they can receive and enjoy the experience. Sensory Being Consultants Zoe and Freya regularly threw objects away during our explorations with them but were always interested in exploring them again. Their throwing did not represent rejection.

Sensory processing disorder

Sensory processing disorder (SPD) is when our nervous system finds it difficult to interpret and organise the information received from the senses. It might be that the way we respond to a sound seems painful for example. When processing is disordered, the brain cannot do its most important job of organising our sensory messages. When we receive information from each sense it is translated via specialised nerves, which interpret that sensation, and then sent via the central nervous system to our brain. Our brain consists of sensory pathways which are created from sensory information received. These pathways are created from repetitive exposure to sensory stimuli. For people with SPD these pathways may have difficulty interpreting the information.

For someone who experiences sound as being painful, it may be that their brain is receiving and processing all the auditory information in that environment but finding it difficult to filter out the sounds which are not important. All are being processed so all the sounds in the environment could seem like they are on full volume meaning the brain has found it difficult to organize them. Individuals with SPD can easily become overwhelmed in response to their sensations.

Becky Lyddon: Founder of Sensory Spectacle, seven years' practical experience supporting young people with PMLD, Autism, learning difficulties, physical disabilities.

Overload

Processing capacity

Sensory systems may shut down if they are overloaded. Too many competing stimuli can mean the brain shuts down the receiving channels on some of the information so that it is able to focus its processing capabilities on the remaining incoming information. People can feel they are being generous by offering an individual lots and lots of different sensory experiences all at once, and for some people this will be generosity, but for others it will be overwhelming.

Fight or flight

Sensory overload is often very frightening. Once our systems are overloaded and begin to shut down, we become disorientated in the world. Our senses, on a fundamental level, are for the finding of nourishment food/love and for the avoidance of becoming someone else's food. When our senses overload, our system goes into an emergency state and the fight-or-flight response is triggered in our brain.

In order that we might win the fight, or flee as fast as possible, other systems are closed down to ensure maximum energy and effort goes into the fighting or flighting. This means we cannot think clearly, we cannot process information, and we cannot take in new information. We become a bundle of terror trying to survive.

If you have inadvertently triggered fight or flight in a person, you cannot explain to them that these toys are fun; you cannot demonstrate that the lights are actually pretty or the sound is funny. It is not that your explanations are not good or your demonstrations are not accurate, it is that it is *not physically possible* for them to take them onboard. The systems they would ordinarily use to process the information you are offering have been shut down in order to prioritise their personal safety. Once fight or flight is triggered, information about the stimulus that triggered the response is not relevant to the individual experiencing it. Their thinking is forward looking only. They are working out how to attack or how to flee. Telling them that whatever has triggered the response is not a danger to them is pointless. Similarly, explanations about how one ought to respond to the situation are equally as pointless. Once fight or flight is triggered, the individual is not in a position to learn; they are not capable of remembering new information or processing your insights. All they can do is fight or flee.

The kindest thing to do for someone in sensory overload is to not get in their way. Allow them to flee to a place of safety without experiencing the need to fight their way out. This could mean assisting them in withdrawing from the situation and finding them somewhere with low sensory stimulation where they can recover. It could mean you withdrawing the stimulation you are offering and allowing them time without excess stimulation to recover. Gradually the hormones released as a part of the fight-or-flight response will clear from their system and they will be again able to engage.

Overload is not always obvious

A fight-or-flight reaction is a very clear signal that too much sensory stimulation has been provided to a person. However, not all experiences of sensory overload will be displayed in fight-or-flight reactions. Some people experiencing overload simply shut down, cease responding, and distance themselves internally by becoming withdrawn and passive. Noticing these responses is harder, as they are less obvious in themselves, but if you have built up a good picture of how the person you support normally is, then you will be able to notice when there are differences to the norm and question what might be causing these differences. Sensory overload is one possible answer.

Overload is not always a result of overstimulation

Sensory modalities are not only shut down by physical overstimulation; they can also shut down in response to stress. You may notice the sensory abilities of the person you support fluctuate in response to times of stress in their lives. It is important, as you watch for their responses and abilities, to not assume they will be the same as on previous occasions; you have to do your detective work afresh each day, each hour, each moment.

Calming touch

The judicious use of touch can help someone who is in a state of stress. Touch plays a big role in the development of our ability to feel secure and safe in another person's presence. Scientists investigating touch have found it instigates structural changes in the developing brain. Nurturing touch has been shown to be a favourable influence on the way the brain matures and also to decrease stress levels.[5] A stressed individual (Sensory Being or Linguistic Being) may welcome an early developmental easy-to-process touch experience – for example, a hand laid firmly on the shoulder.

Take-away tips

- Touch can be a very counterintuitive sense when thinking about how best to begin. Soft, gentle touches can be distressing and irritating.

- Touching and being touched is important to our physical and mental health.

- Rejection of touch should be investigated; it does not always mean that a Sensory Being does not want to experience touch.

- Sensory overload can cause our sensory systems to shut down or trigger a fight-or-flight response.

- Respecting a person's sensory abilities and preferences is likely to lead to a progression in the number and types of experiences they are willing to engage with.

- Pushing a person to take part in experience is likely to lead to a rejection of those experiences.

Part B: tactile experiences

Exploring the scope of tactile experience

We have explored some of the interesting territory around the counterintuitiveness of tactile experience. Here we focus back in on what sort of touches we might be offering. Touch is such a fantastic sense to explore. The touch organ on the body, i.e. the skin, is the biggest of the sensory organs, so we have got so many different experiences we can offer – just think how different it is to be touched on the back of your knee compared to the front.

In this chapter, we look first at the touch experiences that are most likely to be most accessible to the most number of Sensory Beings and move on to look at how we can explore different tactile sensations with Sensory Beings who are able to process more complex tactile experiences. We consider this with reference to human touch and touching objects. The end of this chapter is dedicated to erotic touch and offers a note of caution to those who may seek to ban Sensory Beings from indulging in erotic touch.

Human touch

Firm touch

When starting out with touch, begin with a relatively firm, heavy touch, proportionate to the build of the individual you are touching. A firm touch presents a strong message to the brain, carried not just by the touch receptors on the skin, but also by receptors in the tissues and muscles beneath the skin.

Static touch

A firm static touch is a reassuring and clear message to process. A moving touch may be harder for the brain to process as it has to register the sensation whilst simultaneously tracking the movement. Using the words like firm and static makes this type of touching sound clinical or controlling. Think of the firm static touches you experience. These are probably hugs or reassuring shoulder clasps; they are friendly steadying gestures that let you know another person is with you and will support you. These are the sorts of touch experiences that make for a great starting point when using touch with Sensory Beings.

Practitioner insight

One of my students is VERY sensitive to gentle touch – he hates being tickled, patted, stroked, etc. He becomes very agitated and can often be aggressive – lashing out and possibly biting. However, get him in a headlock and rub your knuckles on his head, and he'll do anything you ask of him!! I wasn't sure how he would respond to TacPac (a sensory communication resource), but using a suggestion from another teacher of putting my hand into a sock (like a sock puppet monster) and 'attacking' him with it, I can grab his attention and prepare him for the TacPac objects – it works as his TacPac signifier. When using the objects on him, he prefers me to be 'rough,' and he shows a definite preference for the harder objects. The feathery, 'soft' objects will only be tolerated if they are used in a firm manner. He doesn't usually take items from a member of staff, but during TacPac, he will reach out for the hard objects and explore them.

Moving and rhythmic touch

From firm static touch, we progress to moving touch. Offering touch in a rhythmic fashion is often more easily accepted by people than random touch. Rhythm means people can prepare their systems for what to expect; they can anticipate the experience and get ready to process it. A slow, steady rhythm can be calming. Stress can lead to a reduction in our abilities to process sensory information; the flip side of this is that calmness can mean we are more able to process and respond to experience, so a calming experience can enhance engagement.

Location of touch

We can offer touch to different locations on the body. This can be a good starting point if you are supporting a person who is easily overwhelmed by touch; you can begin with touch in areas of the body that do not have a lot of nerve endings when compared to other locations. You can use your own body to roughly map this out. Think of contrasting areas – for example, the skin on the outside of the upper arm compared to that of the inside of the lower arm. Likewise, if the person you support needs a stronger experience in order to register it, then you might choose to offer touch to a relatively sensitive area of the body – for example, the face or hands.

Containment touch

Drawing on insight from research into the impact of touch in neonates, our smallest Sensory Beings, practitioners have found what they term 'containment touch'[6] to be particularly comforting. An example of containment touch would be to place one hand on the top of a person's head and the other hand over their overlapping hands. It is like a hug, but with less all-over body information to process. Adults with autism report enjoying the sensation of having their head or chest firmly clasped in a containment hold. Containment touch could be a way of offering a person who is unable to cope with the sensation of being hugged the secure feeling of a hug.

Story Massage

Story Massage is part of the sensory curriculum in many special schools. Sensory coordinators find that the combination of positive, nurturing touch with the familiar words of stories helps encourage communication and engagement even among those with the most profound disabilities. It can also be used in intensive interaction with coloured lights and music to accompany the activity.

Story Massage is based on ten simple massage strokes that are applied, through clothes, to any part of the body that is acceptable and appropriate for the individual making it suitable for all ages and abilities. The strokes are used to 'illustrate' the words of a favourite song or story – or used to create a personalized story for the individual. It is such a simple concept and can easily be shared with parents as a fun, touch-based activity in the family home.

Mary Atkinson: award-winning complementary therapist and author of four books on massage. www.storymassage.co.uk

Touch and objects

Objects

In addition to human contact, touch can be the passive touching of an object or the active exploration of one. If we are looking to engage a person in touch, then thinking about the processing of tactile experience is a good place to start.

Tactile experience is continuous

Our skin is continuously picking up messages about what it is touching and sending them to the brain for processing. Our experience of touch is therefore ongoing – unlike, for example, our experience of sight, which stops if we close our eyes. This means that for a touch experience to stand out and become focused upon, it needs to present a stronger, or contrasting, message to the multitude of messages already being processed.

Think about what you are touching now. Until I set you the challenge, you were not fully aware of your body, but now you can feel your toes in your shoes, your arms resting against the table, your fingers holding this book, your hair brushing your neck, the pressure of the seat beneath your bottom, your teeth against your tongue, your ear lobes, your back, the warmth of the sun on your face, or a cool breeze. . .so many touch sensations are available to you in the moment.

Prioritising tactile experience

We prioritise the tactile signals we pay attention to so that we can focus on the knowledge that is useful to us – for example, so that we can feel to do up a button. The person you support may be experiencing all the messages at once. Their brain will not necessarily focus on the information we would see as relevant; instead, it is likely to be drawn towards whichever signal is strongest. Therefore, rather than start with something soft and gentle, it is advisable to begin the tactile exploration of objects with a Sensory Being by choosing objects that will send big signals. Objects that are rough, heavy, sharp and hard send the boldest messages to the brain, shouting "I am here, you can feel me."

Safety

Safety is, of course, essential. I am not for a minute suggesting you share sharp blades as a touch experience, or offer people their choice of a drawing pin to explore. Rather, evaluate the touch experiences that safe-to-share objects have to offer. Choose something that is likely to send a message that will be received loud and clear.

Heavy

Weighty objects are good for sending strong messages. The risk with such objects is that they can fall on a person and hurt them, but weight does not have to be experienced in the vertical plane – for example, by placing something heavy on a person so that it presses down upon them. Weight can be experienced horizontally by placing a heavy object on the floor and providing the person you support the opportunity to push against it. Alternatively, you can suspend a heavy object using bungee cord or rope (being sure to tie everything in place securely) so they can experience moving it in space without risk of it falling onto them.

Rough

Rough objects are easy to find. Sandpaper is a great example as it comes in different grades – what a super opportunity: grab a long cardboard tube and glue different grades of sandpaper to the outside to create a range of experiences to explore. Create your own rough objects together – for example, by sinking gravel in Plaster of Paris to create a rough, bumpy surface to be explored with hands or feet.

Sharp

Sharp objects are not an automatic safety no-no. There are lots of examples of spikes that provide resistance but are unlikely to puncture the skin. Pet shops often have spikey balls that will endure a good deal of exploring before showing any signs of wear and tear. The laundry aisle of your local supermarket may also be a good place to hunt for spikes, as dryer balls are spikey, hard and durable. For smaller balls, you may be able to thread them on a rope and secure them to a fixed point so that they can be explored safely without risk of getting swallowed.

Feet

Exploring texture with the feet is a great way of extending a person's interest in the world and also of sharing stimuli that might be risky to explore with the hands. For example, pressing the feet into earth can be a gorgeously rich sensory experience. Exploring earth with the hands can also be a wonderful experience, but it is more likely to end up in the mouth. Similarly, rough textures fixed to boards to create a path are a great way to safely explore objects which, if held in the hands, could quickly and inadvertently become weapons!

Tapping into the somatosensory system through touch

Our somatosensory system is vying for a position as the Sensory Project's eighth sense, but for now I am sticking resolutely to seven, and so we will sneak it in again here. The somatosensory system registers pain, itchiness, temperature and pressure. We have talked about weighty objects which offer the opportunity to experience pressure. We do not want to cause pain, and so we are left with temperature. As you look for engaging tactile experiences, consider ones offering different temperatures.

There are plenty of simple, cheap ways to offer temperature-related touch – for example: hot water bottles; re-usable hand warmers in which a small metal disc is flexed to trigger an exothermic chemical reaction, which can be reversed by submerging the handwarmer in boiling water for a few minutes; or simply bowls of water at different temperatures. See Figure 10.4.2 for a visually beautiful way of creating an entrancing object for sensory-being that sends a strong message to the somatosensory system.

Nature and the senses

The Sensory Trust is a national charity concerned with: making outdoor spaces accessible, usable and enjoyable for everyone; connecting people with nature and the outdoors regardless of age, disability or background; ensuring people can have meaningful experiences that better connect them to the natural world.

When out enjoying nature we often rely heavily on our visual sense, it is important to make sure we bring all of our senses into play and really take in our surroundings. When running outdoor workshops we often ask people to find certain textures, sometimes matching them up with ones we have brought along, frequently I have these pointed out to me from some distance. Are you sure that is the same texture I will ask, let's check, when we go to it and actually touch it, it can sometimes be quite different. I don't know why there can be a reluctance to touch, perhaps it is a permissive thing, people are unsure whether it is ok to touch plants, flowers, rocks. As long as you are respectful they really don't mind!

Physically connecting with objects through touch can give us so much more of a sensory explanation, the texture, the temperature, the weight, the fragility. Instinctively we touch with our hands, we reach out and hold, however it is often our least sensitive part of our body and touching with other body parts can give us a more genuine understanding of the object. So get out and really feel things in nature, feel the rough and the smooth, the wet and the dry, sit on something bumpy, cover yourself in sand, get stuck in and treat yourself to a great sensory touch experience.

Lynsey Robinson: Inclusive Designer at the Sensory Trust. www.sensorytrust.org.uk

Begin with passive, static, tactile experience of objects

As with the buildup of human-to-human touch, we can begin by placing an object against the skin of the person we are supporting for them to experience in a passive way. We will then make a choice: do we move the object around or keep it still? There are arguments for doing both, and the right answer to this question for you will depend on the person you are supporting and how they are feeling in the moment in which you present the experience.

Advantages of moving an object

If I place a spiky ball against your skin, your brain may receive messages from your skin saying "I feel spikes." Once this message is sent, it may not be sent again, as it is the presentation of the spikes that triggers the message. Once the spikes are against our skin, we do not feel 'spiked'; we feel a steady pressure, which is a different sensation. If I roll the spiky ball against a small patch of your skin, your brain may receive a succession of messages from this area of the skin saying "I feel spikes, I feel spikes, I feel spikes." The continued repeated messages have more chance of being processed than the single message.

Advantages of keeping an object still

If I place a hard shape against your fingertips, your brain may receive a message from the skin on your fingertips saying "I feel something hard." If this sparks the curiosity of your brain, it may send a message back asking the fingertips for more information. If, by the time this message reaches the fingertips, the object is gone, the brain will lose interest. Asking your sensory systems and brain to work in synchrony to simultaneously feel and track an object is asking them to do two things at once, which might be a little cheeky as a first request. Presenting them with a single, consistent stimulus offers them the chance to focus their attention and organise themselves to work together so that they can process the message.

Which is the right thing to do? As ever, that will depend on the person you are supporting. However, it may also depend on the nature of the object. It is also likely that there is an element of balance involved; for example, rolling the spikey ball over a small area of skin asks the brain to attend to that area, whereas rolling it from head to toe over someone's body asks the brain to race about the place.

Active exploration of objects

People with the physical ability to actively explore touch experience will benefit from the opportunity to explore objects with engaging tactile properties. These are likely to be objects that are hard, sharp, rough, heavy, etc., but will extend to objects that have all sorts of other interesting tactile properties. Think about objects that are slippery, slimy, gungy, soft, fluffy; objects that slip through your fingers, like sand or grains; and objects that encourage movement along them – for example, ropes or the sandpaper tube I described on page 101.

Often the first part of our bodies utilised to actively explore tactile experience is the mouth. The lips and tongue have a high density of nerve endings and so are a brilliant choice to make when looking to explore how something feels.

Erotic touch

A connection with the sensory world is essential for well-being and enjoyment of life. People tend to overlook the majority of their sensory experiences, perhaps picking out just a few which they identify as bringing pleasure: favourite foods, music and sex.

Erotic touch is a sensory experience people pour huge amounts of time, effort and money into finding. It is valued very, very highly in life. Having a disability should not mean a person is prevented from exploring this experience. To forbid access to sexuality is to forbid someone from a fundamental part of being human.

Clearly it is not appropriate to be offering erotic touch to anyone other than a consenting partner, so it is unlikely to be something we can offer to a Sensory Being. However, erotic touch is often something that people supporting Sensory Beings attempt to prevent.

Linguistic Beings have an understanding of the social world and the appropriateness of different types of touch within that world which is not relevant to the experience of a Sensory Being. Rather than try to impose our world on theirs, by attempting to enforce rules which they do not have the capacity to understand, we should look for ways to allow them to be and express themselves within our world, so that both worlds are able to co-exist.

It is possible to enforce rules and stop people from touching themselves in an erotic way. We can scold a person in such a way that they grow to fear erotic touch and self-regulate. If we do this without thinking, we may consider that our 'discipline' has been understood and the person has consented to follow our rules. This assumes they have understood the social context, understood our desires, understood that there are consequences to their actions and understood that these particular actions fall into a category that is banned. It assumes a lot. The alternative interpretation of a Sensory Being ceasing behaviour after being continuously banned from taking part in it is a more brutal behaviourist interpretation, which may have consequences to that individual's well-being far beyond the cessation of a particular behaviour. Learned helplessness could be one of those consequences.

Learned helplessness

The classic learned helplessness experiments were conducted by Martin Seligman at the University of Pennsylvania in the late 1960s and early 1970s.[7] Seligman was interested in the impact of depression on behaviour. He conducted an experiment which was to become famous using dogs.

Seligman's dogs were split into three groups. Group one experienced the experimental equipment, which consisted of a harness, the room and the apparatus within it. Group one did not receive any electric shocks. Group two dogs were put in harnesses and given random electric shocks, but there was a button in the room they could press with their paws to stop the shocks. Group three received shocks at the same time as group two but had no access to the button, so their shocks stopped only when the dogs in group two pressed the button.

These same dogs were then placed in a shuttle box, and this box was divided by a low fence. On one side of the fence, the floor was metal and delivered an electric shock; on the other side, there was no shock. The dogs were placed on the metal floor side of the box and an electric shock was administered. The dogs from the first two groups quickly leapt the fence, escaping the shock. The dogs in the final group, who had learned that there was nothing they could do to escape the shock in the first permutation of the experiment, laid down and whimpered when the shock was administered. They did not try to escape.

When we crush someone's spirit in one activity, it remains crushed and impacts all that they do.

We are not administering electronic shocks when we ban someone from an activity. But if a person learns that no matter how hard they try, something they desire is not possible, their learning is the same as that of the dogs in the third group. They learn that effort is not rewarded; they learn that they are power-less, and they are liable to give up effort in other situations too.

Sensory Beings are at increased risk of developing learned helplessness. It is all too easy to support someone in a way that fosters the development of learned helplessness not only by defeating their spirit as described above, but by doing tasks for them which they are able to do themselves. We should always seek to support a person in a way that honours their experience of the world and allows them all the agency within that experience that it is possible for them to manifest.

Learned helplessness

The effect of learned helplessness has been shown very clearly in people too, and it is associated with apathy, depression, anxiety, phobias and loneliness. It is also worth mentioning that this kind of emotional difficulty over time has proven to weaken the immune system and worsen physical disease. In other words, having a feeling of control over our environment directly impacts a person's chance to live a full and happy life.

This is important because the environment our children find themselves in could easily be promoting learned helplessness, with all of the negative consequences that it brings.

Extract from "Fighting back from learned helplessness,"
http://rettuniversity.org/fighting-back-helplessness by
Jennie Simmons: Psychologist, Researcher, Complimentary
Therapist and mother to a daughter with Rett Syndrome.

Jennie goes on to talk about how she prevents learned helplessness by taking steps to ensure her daughter is not a passive recipient in her own life.

Creative erotica

If you support a Sensory Being who is interested in providing their own erotic touch, I am sure you can think of a creative solution for how they can be allowed to do this, or a not-so-creative one – for example, being allowed private time in their room. If you are concerned that their interest in erotic touch is overwhelming their ability to be interested in the wider world, then, instead of looking at how you can ban them from exploring their passion, hunt for experiences that might tempt them away from it. Erotic touch is hard to beat in terms of a purely sensory experience; our bodies are wired to seek it out, and they reward us with lots of pleasure hormones for completing erotic activities. Good luck finding something that beats it!

Take-away tips

- How we touch a person can increase or decrease their likelihood of being able to process and respond to our touch.

- Heavy, rough, sharp objects can (safely facilitated) be good starting points for touch.

- Touch does not belong to the hands alone; we can experience touch anywhere on our bodies. Think about offering the Sensory Being you support touch experiences to different locations on their body.

- Consider how the facilitation of an object may alter a Sensory Being's ability to process its presence – for example, pressure on an object, moving an object, presenting an object in a rhythmic way.

- Sensory Beings have as much right to the pleasures of erotic touch as Linguistic Beings.

- Be extremely careful if you are acting to try and prevent a Sensory Being from doing something. Learned helplessness is very easy to acquire and extraordinarily damaging to a person's quality of life.

Notes

1   Kulkarni, A. et al. (2010) Massage and touch therapy in neonates: The current evidence. *Indian Paediatrics* Vol. 47, Pg 771–776, available online at: http://medind. nic.in/ibv/t10/i9/ibvt10i9p771.pdf
2   Ockenden, J. (2006) Developing a culture of engagement in a service supporting adults with profound and multiple learning difficulties. *PMLD Link* Vol. 18, No. 3, Issue 55, Pg 3–7.

3   McInnes and Treffry (1982) *Deaf-Blind Infants and Children a Developmental Guide.* Milton Keynes Open University Press.

4   Bond, C. (2002) Positive touch and massage in the neonatal unit: A British approach. *Semin Neonatol* Vol. 7, Pg 477–486.

5   Schore, A. N. (2001) The experience-dependent maturation of an evaluative system in the cortex. In Pibram, K. H. (ed.) *Brain and Values: Is a Biological Science of Values Possible?* (pp. 337–358). Mahwah, NJ: Erlbaum; Schore, A. N. (2001) Effects of a secure attachment relationship on right brain development, affect regulation, and infant mental health. *Infant Mental Health Journal* Vol. 22, Nos. 1–2, Pg 7–66.

6   Bond, C. (2002) Positive touch and massage in the neonatal unit: A British approach. *Semin Neonatol* Vol. 7, Pg 477–486, available online at: www.careperinatologia.it/lavori/L33.pdf

7   Seligman, M. E. P. (1972). Learned helplessness. *Annual Review of Medicine* Vol. 23, No. 1, Pg 407–412.

8

Stimuli for the proprioceptive and vestibular senses

Part A of this chapter contains an introduction to your proprioceptive and vestibular senses, which includes information about how important they are to our lives and why they are worth exploring with Sensory Beings.

Part B of this chapter looks at the early proprioceptive and vestibular experiences we are likely to encounter, and how these can inform our choices of starting experiences for exploring proprioception and vestibulation with Sensory Beings.

Part A: an introduction to proprioception and vestibulation

Here we reflect on our own proprioceptive and vestibular experiences to help us understand the role these senses play in our lives. Proprioception and vestibulation are subconscious senses, leading some people to overlook their potential for exploration with Sensory Beings. We will discuss why they are worth exploring.

Proprioception and vestibulation help us to know where our body is and where it is going. Imagine for a moment *not* knowing where your body is and how it is moving: how strange that would be, how disorientating, how alarming.

Sensory Beings whose senses are in the early stages of development, or whose senses are waning, or whose sensory processing is in some way disordered, may not have access to concrete proprioceptive and vestibular information to orientate and quite literally find themselves. Finding ways to stimulate proprioception and vestibulation gives people the chance to practice processing and responding to proprioceptive and vestibular signals.

Proprioception

Your proprioceptive sense tells you where your body is in space. Think about your body now; if you are someone whose proprioceptive sense is functioning, you know where your feet are, where your legs are, where your back, your bottom, your elbows are, and so on. For some of these body parts, perhaps you are currently receiving tactile information about their location – for example, your feet may be pressing against the floor. But for other parts of your body, your knowledge about their location comes purely from your proprioceptive sense. For example, close your eyes: do you know where your nose is? You are not receiving tactile information about your nose, yet you have a clear sense of where it is; that sense is your proprioception in action.

You can test your proprioception by placing a glass of water on a table and turning your back. Now, with your back turned, reach around and pick up the glass. You are not looking at where the glass is. You cannot hear, taste or smell where the glass is, and you do not feel your way along the table to find it. You have a sense of where the glass is, as you just put it down, and you have a sense (your proprioceptive sense) of where your hand and arm are in space, so you are able to bring your hand to the glass.

You may have had an experience of your proprioception dipping. Our sensory abilities are not fixed; they vary, over time and day to day, influenced by a number of factors, including illness, tiredness and ageing. The experience you have probably had is just as you were falling asleep, or as you were waking up, you felt like you were falling.

The sensation of falling on the boundaries of sleep is triggered by a momentary dip in proprioceptive awareness: for a second, you do not know where your body is. People who experience this react with alarm. It is frightening to not know where you are in space. There is a sudden intake of breath, and hands reach out to slap against the bed. In the absence of proprioceptive awareness, we resort to the next best sense in that moment for orientating ourselves: our sense of touch. Imagine living feeling like this all the time. Opportunities to feel where you are in space would be very reassuring.

The extraordinary case of Ian Waterman

In 1971, Ian Waterman caught something which he first took to be the flu but which turned out to be a disease of the central nervous system. Within days, Mr Waterman had lost all of his tactile and proprioceptive nerves, meaning he could no longer feel the sensation of touch or know where his body was in space. The result of this catastrophic loss was complete paralysis. Mr Waterman's motor systems and physical body were unharmed by the disease, but without his tactile or proprioceptive senses, he was unable to move.

Ian Waterman is an extreme case that serves to demonstrate the fundamental importance of our tactile and proprioceptive systems. I have often been an eavesdropper on conversations where people discuss which sense they would least like to lose. People usually plump for sight or hearing, believing these to be the senses they are most dependent on. Creating a hierarchy of the senses can be entertaining as an after-dinner conversation but has little practical application in life. All our senses are of extreme importance to us, and all contribute enormously to our ability to function in, and to understand, the world.

Mr Waterman is a superb example of how fantastically flexible the brain is able to be. He did not regain his sense of touch or of proprioception, but he did regain his ability to move: by learning to control his muscles using his sense of sight. In essence, he created new wiring connecting his sense of sight to the movement centers in his brain – 'getting wired' anew.

If you are curious to find out more about Mr Waterman, I suggest looking up the 1998 BBC Horizon documentary about him entitled *The Man Who Lost His Body*, which can be found on YouTube.

Vestibulation

Your vestibular sense tells you about your movement and balance. If the room you are sitting in now was somehow magically lifted up and placed on the back of a truck and driven away at speed, although nothing in the room changes (imagine the curtains are closed so that visually everything is the same), you would know you were moving. You would be able to feel the motion. It is your vestibular sense that brings you that information. Similarly, it is your vestibular sense that helps you to know up from down and is the sense you call on to help you balance.

Ménière's disease

Ménière's disease is a vestibular disorder. Dr Sarah Bell, who researches the experience of people with Ménière's, shares what it can be like to have a vestibular system that is not working correctly. Dr Bell's testimony powerfully demonstrates just how important our vestibular system is to our everyday functioning and well-being.

Imagine a world that is almost constantly in motion, where even moments of physical stillness can be punctuated by sensations of drifting, floating, spinning or more severe forms of imbalance. Imagine walking down the street and being taken off guard by a bicycle bell, a passing bus or a barking dog. You unexpectedly fall to the floor in a vertigo attack; the brain, unsure what is going on, tries to respond to the spinning, which manifests in sickness and, for some, loss of bowel control. People walk past you, silently (or verbally) passing judgment on what appears to them to be a response to excessive alcohol. In that moment, you can barely move or talk; you simply try to keep your body as still as possible until you can get help, or until the intensity of the vertigo attack passes.

Living with the constant fear and unpredictability of such attacks, coupled with the mind games created by a world seemingly in motion (which few others can relate to), can be deeply debilitating. In our recent study (Bell et al., 2015), this was highlighted by individuals living with Ménière's disease; a chronic, progressive vestibular disorder, defined by episodes of severe vertigo, aural fullness (pressure within the inner ear), tinnitus and fluctuating hearing loss – in one or both ears. Affecting approximately 120,000 people in the UK, the condition is not well known and there is no cure, rendering affected individuals particularly isolated and vulnerable. A key part of learning to manage its many manifestations is to understand how deeply integrated the vestibular system is with the wider bodily senses. This is essential, both for negotiating the many sensory 'triggers' of imbalance – be they visual, auditory or proprioceptive – but also for 'grounding' the body as the world starts to move. Touch, in particular, is central for distinguishing elements in the environment that are objectively moving from those that seem to be shifting as a result of vestibular impairment.

Dr Sarah Bell: Research Fellow at the University of Exeter.

Bell, S. L., Tyrrell, J. and Phoenix, C. (2015) *Living With Ménière's Disease*. Key findings booklet. European Centre for Environment and Human Health, University of Exeter Medical School, Truro. www.ecehh.org/wp-content/uploads/2015/01/Ménières-research-findings-booklet.pdf

It is worth exploring the subconscious senses

Proprioception and vestibulation are subconscious senses; we do not overtly know we are using them. When we see, we can open and close our eyes; seeing is a conscious act, one we decide to start and stop. Proprioception and vestibulation are ongoing subconscious acts. This subconsciousness can lead to us thinking of them as less important than the famous five senses we were all taught about as children. Dr Bell's testimony above clearly demonstrates the importance of our vestibular sense, as does the story of Ian Waterman (reference to box) with regards to our proprioceptive abilities.

As well as the innate worth of these subconscious senses, there is a pragmatic argument for considering their exploration with Sensory Beings. It is likely that the Sensory Being you support has impairments to some of their conscious sensory systems. Perhaps they experience a degree of blindness and a level of hearing impairment. What if they have an absolutely brilliant sense of proprioception?

We want to give everyone the chance to play to their natural strengths. If we limit the experiences we offer to people to just those relating to the famous five senses, we miss out on the opportunity to enable them to explore other skills they might have. As with all of the senses, looking at the development of these senses will give us clues as to experiences we might like to facilitate for the Sensory Being we are supporting.

Take-away tips

- Disorders or impairments to proprioception and vestibulation have a significant impact on a person's life.

- Proprioception tells you where your body is in space; to not know where your body is in space is extremely alarming.

- Your vestibular sense tells you about your own movement and balance; without it, you can feel disorientated and even experience motion sickness.

- Providing stimulation to subconscious senses such as proprioception and vestibulation can allow Sensory Beings to develop and display their talents.

Part B: proprioceptive and vestibular experiences

As with the chapters on our conscious senses, here you will find examples of the sorts of early proprioceptive and vestibular experiences that provide a good starting point for our exploration of these senses with Sensory Beings. Here we also look at how we can support Sensory Beings to use their conscious senses to help them understand the information received from their proprioceptive and vestibular senses.

Early proprioceptive and vestibular experiences

Through our discussion of the five famous senses, we have seen that many senses become active prior to birth. Although a developing fetus may be receiving information through its proprioceptive and vestibular systems without information from other sensory systems – for example, touch and sight – to relate this information to the experience of these sensations has little meaning. Consider: a fetus may take in the pinky tones of the light coming into the womb and begin to practice seeing the colour red. This information about redness can be directly applied to the world outside the womb. However, a fetus in the womb may experience the sensation of moving forwards quickly, but without seeing that this surging feeling brings you closer to an object, or without feeling that the movement brings you into contact with an object, the sensation itself holds no meaning.

As both our proprioceptive and vestibular senses are strongly related to our awareness of our own movement, through this chapter we will explore them together and link our explorations to information gained through the other sensory systems.

Soothing experiences

We can think of the early proprioceptive and vestibular experiences a fetus will have had the chance to experience; these lead us to ideas for experiences that are soothing. For example, in the womb we will have experienced the rocking motion of our mother walking, and we will also have experienced the containment of the amniotic sack, especially in the third trimester of pregnancy when life in the womb was more of a squeeze.

Opportunities to be rocked and cocooned are likely to be soothing sensory experiences for people. Being gently swung in a hammock is ideal as it incorporates both rocking and cocooning. Many parks in the UK have nest swings which offer a similar experience and can be used by people who might not be able to hold their own bodies up in order to use traditional swings.

Tuning our senses to the world

Our proprioceptive and vestibular experiences begin to carry meaning when we emerge into the world and can understand that the sensation of forward means we get closer to objects that were previously far away, or when we can understand that the sensation of up-ness relates to our balancing upon the surface of the planet.

Sensory experiences that offer the opportunity to practice relating our proprioceptive and vestibular experiences to the real world around us can help us to tune those senses in so that they match up to reality. The manner of these experiences will depend on the physical abilities of the person you are supporting. For some people it could be balancing on a beam, for others it could be looking one way and then looking another.

The person you support may enjoy feeling different sorts of movement – for example, moving forwards and backwards, moving in circles, spinning, and moving up and down. If you can partner these experiences with bold experiences from other senses, this will help them to orientate themselves in the world. For example, tie a red balloon to a door handle (hopefully you have a white panel door, not a red one, so that the balloon stands out boldly in the visual field), and then support the person in moving towards the balloon and backwards away from the balloon.

A typically developing person works out what their vestibular and proprioceptive signals mean through romping around and exploring: children roll down hills, twist swings up and spin around and around on them, slide down slides, climb up on the sofa and leap off. All of these activities, so common in childhood, shake the vestibular system up and give us lots of information about where we are (often through bumps and bruises: "Ouch! Ah . . . *That's* where my head is!")

Offering vestibular input

A person who has not been able to explore the world of movement and balance on their own starts off on a back foot with their ability to interpret the signals they receive from their vestibular system. You can help them to make up this ground by creating experiences that allow them to have some of these sensations. Appreciating that the person you support may not be someone for whom it is appropriate to roll down a hill or leap from a sofa onto a pile of cushions, I encourage you to invent smaller, safer versions of these experiences – for example, use an old pair of tights or a piece of bungee cord to make a bouncy swing for an arm or a leg. By providing support through the use of something elastic, you take away the need for them to be able to hold their own limb up, but with a little movement, either from themselves or from you, they will be able to experience the sensation of swinging.

Practitioner: I tried this idea!

I have a lovely young man in my class who does try to rock his body, but it is exhausting for him and not always very safe. Due to his physical needs, enabling him to access equipment or to roll on the classroom floor is difficult.

I made a sling with a bright pair of tights and let him explore it. I put his arm into it and swung it gently. His face lit up. We did this with his legs whilst he was seated in his chair, and it was met with grins, laughter and excitement.

After repeating this for a few days, just the sight of the tights brought movement and rotation to his wrists. He reaches out for them, it is just a slight movement, but full of meaning for him and for me.

Use your head

Experiences that involve the head are particularly important as the vestibular system is based in the small canals of our ears. For a wheelchair user, the opportunity to move over undulating ground gives a little of the uppy-downy sensations that climbing up and sliding down a slide provide for able-bodied people. Accessible playground equipment is developing all the while, and wheelchair-accessible swings and roundabouts exist. There is even a team in America looking to develop wheelchair-accessible roller coasters.

Supporting proprioceptive understanding

Wrapping, brushing and massage are all great ways of giving information through your tactile sensory system about where the body is in space. Sensory Beings can partner this information with the information they are receiving from their proprioceptive systems and use it to understand where their bodies are. If a Sensory Being has poor proprioception, they may well feel anxious: it's unnerving to not know where your body is in space. Providing these sorts of experiences is a good way to relieve that anxiety.

Here are a few other ways to give tactile information to support a Sensory Being's understanding of their proprioceptive input:

You can buy stretch fabric bags for zipping people into! It is easy to buy stretchy fabric from a haberdashers. You could make a bag, or even just a simple loop of stretchy fabric to wrap around a person's shoulders or legs so that they can have that enclosed sensation and feel the presence of their own body pressing against the gentle resistance of the fabric.

Massage – including massage stories (see box on page 99) – is a great way of being with a person and giving them information about where their body is in space. Massage stimulates the deeper tissues below the skin, meaning more messages are sent to the brain than are sent with touch alone.

Vibration – like massage, vibration is super at stimulating the deeper tissues, and the movement means new messages get sent to the brain on each pulse of the vibration, making it easy for a Sensory Being to tune their attention to and enjoy.

Using a resonance board

A resonance board is a piece of plywood held a few centimetres off the ground by wooden supports. The plywood is thick enough to support a person's weight whilst still being thin enough to flex. This ability to flex means that sounds made against the board resonate through it, enabling a person on the board to both feel and hear the sound.

I use the resonance board with my class of children with complex needs. We tell stories with sound effects on the board. I use rhythm games to initiate communication responses from my students. They are very versatile and I have been able to use them on tabletops or on the laps of children seated in a circle. The adults in the room balance the weight of the boards on their laps, having the board raised up means children who use wheelchairs can participate with their hands more readily and more children can access the board, rather than just having one or two on the board on the floor.

Lisa Parascandolo: Special School Teacher at Willow Dene school in Greenwich.

You can view Dr Lili Neilson's design specifications for resonance boards and download PDF documents showing you how to make your own board at: http://activelearningspace.org/2-uncategorised/30-resonance-board

Visiting www.sense.org.uk/sites/default/files/Resonance-Boards.doc will automatically download you a copy of an article entitled "Resonance boards" by David Brown of California Deaf-Blind Services, which contains further insight and information that you may find useful.

Visiting www.hirstwood.com/wp-content/uploads/2014/08/Clonker-Board-activities.pdf will automatically download you a document of activity ideas for use on resonance boards from Hirstwood Training.

Take-away tips

- A lack of early proprioceptive and vestibular experiences can affect a person's ability to concentrate and learn.

- When providing proprioceptive and vestibular experiences for a Sensory Being, consider what information they will be able to access through their other sensory systems that relates to these experiences. Being able to match information from conscious senses to information from subconscious senses helps us to learn what the sensations from the subconscious senses mean in relation to the world around us.

- Spinning, rocking and cocooning are likely to be popular experiences for Sensory Beings.

9

Foci for Sensory Beings with dementia

This chapter looks at some of the additional considerations you may wish to take into account when hunting for sensory resources for Sensory Beings with dementia. Although focused on dementia, this chapter has many examples that are also pertinent to Sensory Beings who do not have dementia.

Individuals with dementia benefit enormously from the opportunity to engage with the sensory world. Many of the experiences described in the preceding chapters will be perfect for igniting their interest. The suggestions in this chapter should help you to build upon that starting point to create resources beautifully suited to their needs and abilities.[1]

Employ the natural world

Lynsey Robinson from the Sensory Trust, who contributed the insight in the box on page 102 (Nature and the Senses, Chapter 7), makes a particular plea for natural experiences to be offered to people with dementia. Often a person's care needs can mean that they have transitioned from a life where sensory experiences, such as the feel of rain on the skin, were an almost everyday occurrence, to a life where such experiences are a rarity. It is interesting to notice that Coralie Oddy, who is experienced at supporting groups of people with dementia in engaging with activities, chose an outdoor theme to her first sensory story.

Natural-world experiences can also be particularly pertinent to people experiencing high levels of anxiety, as the familiar colours and smells of our environment are innately soothing to us. People often remark on the deep connection children with profound autism seem to have to the natural world. It could be that one of the reasons for this strength of connection is the soothing nature of the experiences for these children.

Nature is restorative

As soon as spring has sprung my son likes to spend all of his time outside. Nature doesn't demand anything from him; it simply provides an abundance of stimulation for his senses. Daryl has sensory processing difficulties; he craves these natural sensations.

The first time he is able to go out into an open space after the long cold winter months have passed is a joyful experience. On his first outing this year he exploded into delighted laughter. He could feel the warmth of the sun and smell the newly mown grass. He could feel the warm breeze and smell the fragrance of earth. I took him to a green space where he could just run, uninterrupted. He was away from the constant demands of a learning environment which his severe Autism and learning disabilities make difficult for him. He was free.

When he is outside he leaves behind the dark evenings and the seasonal affective disorder that touches him more deeply than most. This sense of freedom is so important. His life is so regimented and this provides a rare space in which he can explore at his own pace. He might be drawn to a particular tree with its large trunk of ridged bark and stop to run his hands up and down its surface. He will stop at a ferny hedge to touch the green fronds and breathe in their scent. When he reaches a break in the grass he will pause to grab handfuls of gravel from the path and explore its interesting texture.

All of these experiences help improve Daryl's motor skills and work to regulate his nervous system. This helps him to learn independently in a totally relaxed environment. Watching him I can soothe my own nerves and lose myself in his innocent ballet.

James Gordon: father to a son with profound autism, son to a mother with later-stage dementia and, before life took over, an IT consultant.

Seek out novelty

Novelty of experience can also be important for creating a no-pressure environment for sensory exploration with a person with dementia. Often these experiences are the less natural, more plastic flashing lights and sounds types of experiences, and the newly invented extraordinary gadgets types of experience, although novel items from other cultures and countries would also fit the bill.

The benefit of an entirely novel experience is that there will be no weight of expectation placed on the person to remember something. Stimulating connection with memory through sensory experience is very valuable, but, when you think about it, constantly asking a person who struggles with their memory to remember things is a little like constantly asking someone with paralysis to move. It can lead to the impression that we only value them if they can remember.

By using entirely novel experiences, we send a message to Sensory Beings with dementia that we are interested in who they are now. We are not looking for them to be who they once were – we are allowing them to be who they are now, and when we value their responses in the now, we are communicating that they are valuable to us as who they are now.

The value of the moment for older people

Working in the moment is very valuable for older people. Sometimes an insistence on recalling memories can be stressful. Novel experiences can liberate people to explore and enjoy the moment without placing undue demands on them.

Laura Menzies: Artist, Creative Practitioner and Churchill Fellow.

Sensory experience can be a way to tap into hidden skills

Whilst many Sensory Beings may have limitations on their movement and dexterity, this is not necessarily so for individuals with dementia. We have all heard of the care home resident who no longer remembers their own name but who can still play all of Beethoven's piano concertos. Or the father who does not recognise his son but can still re-wire a plug. That man probably could not tell you how to re-wire the plug. The knowledge for him is no longer in the language centers of his brain, but it is there in his muscle memory; his sensory understanding, and his body, know how to wire the plug.

People with dementia can be sensorially engaged in tasks that are more complex than those that would be accessible for other Sensory Beings. Lynsey gives examples from her work with people with dementia. One lady initially seemed unable to take part in a craft activity, but once she was handed the sheet of stickers, she was able to unpeel every one[2] and stick them onto paper. Another lady was unable to draw a picture herself, but when a facilitator got her started by drawing the trunk of a tree, she went on to fill in the branches with hundreds of carefully drawn leaves.

When looking for activities of this sort, begin by thinking of the sensory nature of the activity – how are you going to capture the person's interest? It will be through their senses: through their prior sensory experience and their current experience. Presenting an activity verbally is less likely to get a response than an activity introduced in a sensory way. Likewise, presenting an activity whose sensory experiences are initially hidden – for example, showing someone the instruments that will be used in a sound-making activity – is less likely to get an engaged response than introducing the activity in a sensory way, e.g. playing a few notes on those instruments. The facilitator who drew the tree trunk introduced the drawing activity in a sensory way, instinctively following a route into sensory-being: they came alongside the person, demonstrated the sensory nature of the task – the colour, the movement – and then subtly stepped back, allowing the person to lead.

Twiddle muffs and completable tasks

There is an increasing awareness about the benefits of providing people in the later stages of dementia with something to do. Many National Health Service (NHS) trusts offer patterns for 'twiddle muffs'; these are knitted or fabric tubes that have different colours and textures and things to fiddle with. Elsewhere, similar items are called twiddle blankets or lap comforters. A collection of peculiar names abounds. But whatever they are called, the point is sensory engagement.

I would advise people creating twiddle muffs to consider the sensory experiences discussed in the previous chapters. It is easy for well-intentioned people to knit a nice soft muff in subtle shades of yellow that the person for whom they are knitting so loved in life. The person ends up with something so soft they can barely feel it and with colours so muted they cannot pick them out. However, if you are able to create something with a bit of rough texture and high-contrast colour, then so much the better.

If you want to make your twiddle muff, it is even better to look for ways to include completable tasks that have great sensory properties.

In their life before dementia, the Sensory Being you are thinking about was probably able to do any number of complex sequential tasks – for example, putting on a coat. This seems so simple to those of us who are able to do it, but if you think about the steps, you begin to realise how complex it is. First, you see the coat as a heap of fabric and recognise it as a coat which can be the shape of a body. You work out from that pile of fabric which is the top and which is the bottom. You also understand that, topologically, this is a garment that has two holes, but it is unlikely that you will be able to see these holes. You must then present the coat to yourself in reverse so as to get your arm down the right hole. To put your arm down the hole, you must visually or tactilely identify the difference between the fabric of the sleeve and the fabric of the coat (which are likely to be the same), then you must swing the coat behind you and repeat this sleeve identification, only this time without looking; then, bringing the two sides of the coat together, you must now match button holes with buttons to fasten the coat.

Someone with dementia may remember that putting on a coat is simple, but their brain is no longer able to remember such a long and complex sequence.

The result is they face something they know to be simple but cannot do. The damage to self-esteem is enormous. If, as their fingers explore the blanket on their lap, they come across a button that is hard and bright and shiny and smooth, on a background that is matt and rough and dark, their fingers may very well be able to hold that button, and instinctually they will look for the button hole or toggle loop and thread it through – then the task will be complete, and they will gain that small piece of satisfaction that comes with a job well done.

Think about their life: what other tasks might you find? Doing up a nut and bolt, undoing one of those slidey chain catches that you get on a door, tying a bow, putting a lid on a jar, snapping a hair clip open and shut. Think about how you might present these tasks to their best sensory advantage: how will you give their senses the best chance at finding them? Things will be on high-contrast backgrounds, contrasting not just in colour but texture too. Things will respond – when they touch them, they will make a noise so they know that they have found something, and they will look different, so they see they are causing something to happen.

If you are supporting someone with dementia, it may be that you are not using the information in the previous chapters as a source for creating a shopping list of sensory items; perhaps you are looking at it as a list of ideas for how you could better present discrete, completable tasks.

The value of the sensory moment for people with dementia

For so long the emphasis in dementia care has been on maintaining skills, yet ultimately families must adjust to what is an inevitable decline in skills for the person with dementia. Practitioners must find ways to help the person with dementia and their families cope in that context and also support them to recognise and celebrate the person who is still there. Moving from an interventionist focus to one that enables a person to live the life they currently find themselves in might lead families and professionals to a more failure-free, fulfilling approach.

Living in the moment, being who we currently are, is immensely valuable. Experiencing sensory stimuli together brings us into the 'right now' and there we find the stimuli we are enjoying together, the people we are sharing the moment with, and the feelings we are collectively experiencing. Being in the moment holds benefits not just for the person with dementia but also for those who care for them.

Rebecca Leighton: Senior Specialist Speech and Language Therapist, Co-Founder of Elenbi consulting and training. www.elenbi.co.uk

121

Take-away tips

- Sensory experiences from nature can be particularly calming.

- Novel experiences give the individual the chance to be appreciated as who they are in the present moment without any pressure to recall past events.

- Sensory experiences can reveal skills that are no longer accessible through verbal communication.

- Providing small, completable tasks and supporting these in a sensory way can be a way of promoting raised self-esteem for Sensory Beings with dementia.

- The current moment is a very precious place; share it in a sensory way to occupy it together with a Sensory Being.

Notes

1   Individuals with dementia are not the only group of people for whom a particular sensory palette can be beneficial. Individuals with Attachment Disorder may benefit from a sensory palette selected from sensory experiences to do with early nurturing care. Individuals with Sensory Processing Disorder may find natural experiences calming and also benefit from the opportunity to encounter a wide range of experiences and practice their responses.
2   Lynsey gave a handy tip with this insight, mentioning that the sticky paper around the stickers had been pre-removed, making the stickers themselves easier to manipulate.

10

Sensory makes

This chapter contains some easy to follow instructions for making some sensory resources. You will find more ideas for things to make in the online Chapter 10 at http://jo.element42.org (follow links to the Sensory-being project).

With each of the makes, there is a brief reference to why it may appeal to the senses, but the reasons for these 'whys' are not presented in detail here as you will have read all about them already in Chapters 3–8.

The materials you need for these makes are all simple, inexpensive and unremarkable in themselves. Do not be fooled by their humble nature. Remember, it is not what a resource is made out of that is important; what is important is what it is like to experience that resource with your senses. An empty drinks bottle can become a thing of great visual beauty. A used deodorant canister can become a tool for creating a deep sensory bond with a Sensory Being. Think with your senses, not with your cognitive understanding of what objects are, and enjoy creating marvellous sensory moments for the Sensory Being/s you support.

Scented massage roller

A scented massage roller is fantastic for stimulating the sense of smell. Choose your scents based on the person you will be sharing this experience with. The pressure delivered through the massaging is a wonderful way to give tactile, somatosensory and proprioceptive stimulation along with the olfactory stimulation provided by the scent. Sharing this experience can be wonderfully calming.

You need: an empty roller ball deodorant, some olive oil, and herbs or essential oils.

1   First you need to wash out the deodorant bottle. To remove the ball, place the deodorant bottle into boiling water; the ball will gradually ease itself

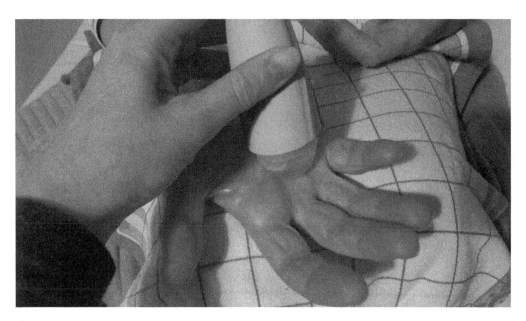

Figure 10.1.1

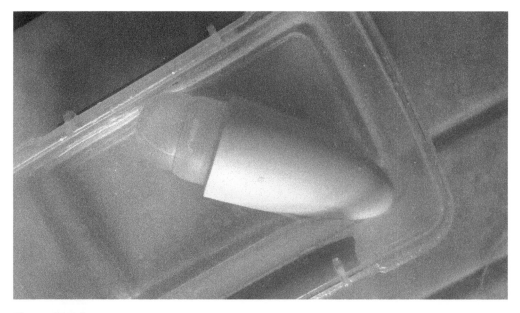

Figure 10.1.2

out of the bottle. Once it is out, you can wash the inside of the bottle and the ball itself thoroughly.

2 Pour olive oil into the empty bottle and add scent, in the form of drops of essential oil, or torn fresh herbs, or dried herbs.

Figure 10.1.3

Figure 10.1.4

3   To replace the ball, simply press it back in situ. If this is difficult to do, you
     may need to warm the plastic that holds the ball in place with a little more
     hot water, but step 2 should be quick to complete, so it is likely that it will
     still be flexible enough. Once completely cooled, it is safe for a responsible
     facilitator to use.

Reflections box

The reflections box is a lovely way to share an activity with a Sensory Being who has very limited physical movement but can engage in activities visually. It can also be great to use with Sensory Beings who have basic physical movement but have become disengaged with activities. Gently watching you

Figure 10.2.1

complete a task with no direct pressure on them to join in can allow them to engage with the task at their own pace.

The reflections box allows you to share the visual pleasure of colouring in with a Sensory Being. When you are choosing colours and patterns to colour, keep in mind the influences we discussed in Chapter 3.

You need: a large, sturdy cardboard box and tin foil. Optional: mirror tiles.

1   Stand the box on its side and cut a large flap into the top of the box.

2   Line the box inside with tin foil, and leave the bottom panel of the box plain.

Figure 10.2.2

3 Glue on mirror tiles wherever you like, but focus especially on the flap you cut and on the outer flaps of the box. You can even hang mirror tiles from thread inside the box; these can be especially nice as they will visually record the movement of your hand as you colour in, jiggling as your pen jiggles the page.

Figure 10.2.3

4   Optional – depending on how stiff the cardboard of your box is, you may choose to use a little wool or thread to hold the flaps open at the right angle.

To share this experience with a Sensory Being, sit next to them and angle the flaps of the box so that the base panel of the box is reflected towards them. Place your colouring in on this base panel and colour. You will enjoy the calming activity of colouring. The Sensory Being will enjoy seeing the gentle movements of your hands and the gradually changing colours reflected in the foil and mirrors.

Bottled wonders

Empty drinks bottles are one of the most versatile resources for creating engaging sensory resources. With so many possibilities, it is not possible to detail them all here, merely to give ideas. Happily, the making involved is always wonderfully simple: you put something in the bottle and screw the lid on tight, which means we need not use up space explaining these makes but instead can utilise it to explore some possibilities. For more examples or more detailed explanations of these makes, please see the online Chapter 10 (go to http://jo.element42.org and follow links to the Sensory-being project).

Remove the labels from the outside of the drinks bottles, fill them with water and add scraps of coloured cellophane to create delightfully visually engaging resources. The water magnifies and intensifies the colours.

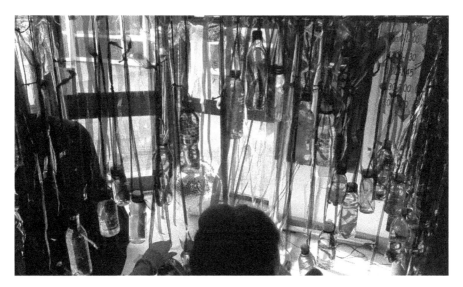

Figure 10.3.1   Suspending the bottles on string or elastic can make them easier and more responsive for Sensory Beings to interact with.

Figure 10.3.2 The water inside the bottle magnifies the feather's details, enabling it to be explored up close.

The weight of the water and the coolness of it stimulate the tactile, proprioceptive and vestibular sensory systems. The movement of the scraps of cellophane within the water means one simple bottle can offer a thousand different visual experiences. Adding a small pebble or a marble to the bottle means that a Sensory Being exploring the resource gets extra feedback as the pebble bumps and rattles against the inside of the bottle.

Frosted bottles are great for putting small lights into. In these photos, you see two empty milk bottles hung on a coat hanger and presented against a home-made backdrop with little colour-changing lights inside.

The backdrop is made from a large cardboard box cut in half and lined with a dark felt; this creates a matt background against which it is easy for Sensory Beings to spot light objects. Being hung on a coat hanger makes the bottles easy to move and slide, meaning a Sensory Being interacting with them can produce a relatively big response with a small movement. In Figure 10.3.5, you can see another milk bottle with a light inside. This time, a face has been added to create an extra visual draw and the bottle is hung from the matt-coloured

Figure 10.3.3

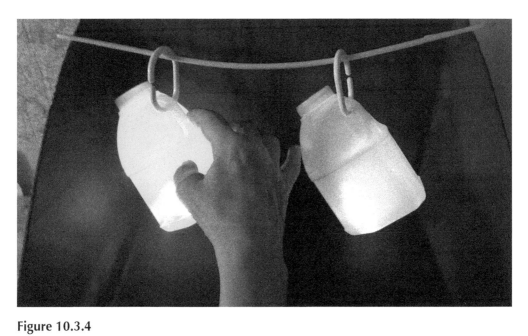

Figure 10.3.4

Figure 10.3.5

backdrop of an umbrella. The Sensory Being Consultants loved this resource, often watching it after their turn with it had finished and reaching out for it.

For Sensory Beings able to grip, squeezing a bottle hard can be a way of experiencing strong, calming vestibular feedback. Creating a bottle diver is a super way to encourage grip and pressure.

Figure 10.3.6

You need: a pen lid or similar shaped item (I have used an empty bubble mixture container) that has no air holes in it, and an adhesive product such as Blu Tack.

1   Fill a bottle with water.

2   Create a little ring of Blu Tack around the open end of the lid.

3   Pop the lid into the bottle, allowing a little water to get inside it. The Blu Tack will pull the open end of the lid down, trapping an air bubble inside.

4   Screw the bottle lid on tight.

Squeezing the outside of the bottle will cause your pen lid diver to descend to the bottom of the bottle, when you release your grip your diver will return to the surface.

If you are unable to get the diver to descend through squeezing, tip the bottle until a single air bubble pops out of the lid. Now try squeezing again. If it is still too hard to get the diver to descend, release another bubble. Be careful – if you release too many bubbles, your diver will simply sink and not resurface.

Interesting ice

If you have the use of a freezer, then ice can be a wonderful sensory-being resource. Smash ice cubes for an interesting texture to explore. Freeze liquid paint, leaving a spoon or a straw dipped into the paint to be used as a handle once the paint is frozen, and then use the lumps of paint ice to create cool pictures.

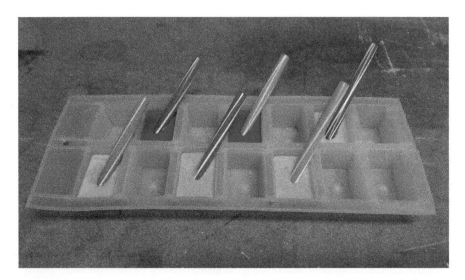

Figure 10.4.1

Figure 10.4.2

Freezing objects into large blocks or balls of ice creates fascinating objects that glisten and shine, that are cool to the touch and that slide away when pressed against. The example in Figure 10.4.2 was created by stuffing a few tinsel remnants into a balloon and then filling that balloon with water and allowing it to freeze. Of course, you can just freeze water in boxes to create ice blocks, but experimenting with different containers can be fun. Try freezing water inside a rubber glove to create an ice hand. If you add glitter and coloured ink into your gloves, they will fall to the fingertips and give your ice hand a fancy manicure. You could also create taste experiences by adding fruit juices or small bits of food – be sure to supervise Sensory Beings exploring taste closely to avoid any choking.

Superb spinners

You will know from Chapter 3 how wonderful our eyes find things that spin. Anything will spin if you hang it from a single point on a fine thread. You may find that some resources you already own become all the more fascinating if you facilitate them in this way for the Sensory Being you support.

Here are two ideas for beautiful spinning objects; they are super simple to make and although one requires a special purchase, I think you will agree it makes something so aesthetically pleasing that it is worth the extra expenditure. As with all visual experiences, think about using a small pen torch to highlight the object and add to the visual interest, and consider lighting and background as you position it for the enjoyment of a Sensory Being.

Figure 10.5.1

You need: silver cardboard, glue, a craft knife or scissors and thread.

1 Glue the silver card together so that both sides are silver.

2 Cut a shape out of the card (I cut a diamond shape).

3 Draw or imagine a line down the middle of the shape. Mark one centimetre along this line from the outer edge of the shape and begin to cut, following the edge of the shape but keeping one centimetre away from it at all times. Cut until you reach the line again. (For me, this meant cutting a > shape.)

4 Now, beginning just a few millimetres below where you began your previous cut, repeat the process but this time cutting away from the line in the opposite direction.

5 Repeat steps 3–4 each time, moving about a centimetre down the central line until there is no space left to cut.

6 Fold the different sections out to make your shape three-dimensional and suspend it from the thread at its highest point.

Figure 10.5.2

Figure 10.5.3

You need: a plastic cocktail bowl (these can often be purchased for as little as a pound), thin wire, Fantasy Film (this can be purchased from craft shops or online via sites like Amazon or eBay – search in the 'craft' section to avoid turning up feature film results. For this make, you want transparent film; opaque films are also available), a glue gun and glue.

Figure 10.5.4

1   Using the wire and the Fantasy Film, create a selection of random shapes and colours.

2   Glue your Fantasy Film creations to the inside of the cocktail bowl using hot glue.

3   Create a handle for your cocktail bowl using wire or thread, and then suspend your bowl from a single point.

The bowl will spin beautifully, and if positioned in the light, it will not only be a beautiful visual experience in and of itself but will cast an array of delightful coloured shadows on the surface beneath. If you are supporting a Sensory Being who uses a lap tray, consider setting this experience up so that the coloured shadows will fall onto their tray.

A smell noodle

Whilst sourcing volatile scents to share with Sensory Beings is relatively easy, finding ways to share pheromone scents can be much harder. Pheromone scents can be wonderfully comforting and can not only provide stimulation in and of themselves, but, through their calming nature, can open up a person's ability to engage with and process other experiences. Creating a smell noodle gives you a way of facilitating pheromone scent experiences for Sensory Beings.

You need: fabric, thread, stuffing, a sewing machine or a needle and patience.

1   Choose a length of fabric to create your smell noodle from. Ordinarily, when choosing fabric as a part of the Sensory Projects, I would be looking for something with wonderful sensory properties of its own, but for the smell noodle you want something that offers low-level stimulation, something soft and plain. You might also like to explore the possibility of textiles supposed to have antibacterial qualities, such as bamboo and rayon fabrics.

2   Cut a piece of fabric wide enough to fold in half and create something approximately the circumference of your arm. The length you choose will be determined by the size of the Sensory Being you are making this for, and how you plan to facilitate the experience. You might choose a short length for a small Sensory Being to hug in bed as they might a teddy bear, or a long length to be worn around the shoulders like a scarf. Fold it so that the top side of the fabric faces inwards and stitch along the long edge and around one end.

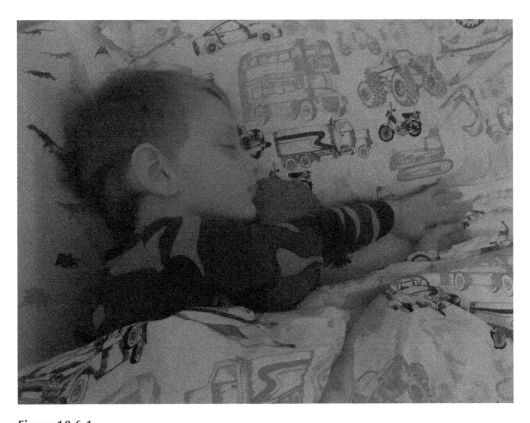

Figure 10.6.1

Figure 10.6.2

Figure 10.6.3

Figure 10.6.4

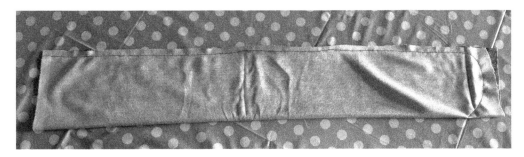

Figure 10.6.5

3 Turn the tube you have made inside out so that the top side of the fabric now faces outwards, and stuff the tube lightly. Remember, the Sensory Being you support may press their face into the noodle, and you want them to be able to breathe through it. Dense stuffing may pose a suffocation hazard. Consider whether it is safe for the Sensory Being you support to use this noodle alone; as a guide, Sensory Beings who are safe sleeping on pillows should be able to use the noodle alone.

4 If you like, you may want to embroider a little face onto your noodle to add a little extra sensory connection.

Facilitating this experience takes consensual preparation from the Sensory Being's nearest and dearest. Ask the person or people closest to the Sensory

Figure 10.6.6

Figure 10.6.7

Being to sleep with the smell noodle in their bed for a few nights. Request that they refrain from wearing any strong-smelling perfumes or deodorants whilst they sleep with the smell noodle. The smell noodle will pick up the person/people's natural odours. Remember, we are looking to harvest pheromone scents, so the noodle may not 'smell' to us when we sniff it after this process as we tend to sniff for volatile scents; but to someone with a close connection to those particular pheromone scents, it will smell very comforting. The scents will need topping up every once in a while, so this process will need repeating after the smell noodle has been used for a while.

Once scented with meaningful pheromone scents, the smell noodle can be used as a comforter during the day. That sensory feeling of nearness to a loved one helps us to feel secure and safe, and when we feel secure and safe, we are better able to engage with the world around us – so it may be that a Sensory Being supported by a smell noodle draped around their shoulders feels more able to engage with other stimulus. It is the smell equivalent to having your hand held.

The smell noodle could be used as a direct focus experience in itself: offered to the Sensory Being to smell, perhaps as part of a conversation about the people of whom it smells.

The smell noodle could be used as a comfort for a Sensory Being falling asleep. We are naturally pack animals and want to sleep together with those to whom we feel connected. The experience of falling asleep alone in the dark is alien to us all, but sleeping with the smell of loved ones can help to mitigate the natural distress we feel at being on our own.

Further reading

If you want even more ideas for sensory resources relevant to Sensory Beings, Flo Longhorn's *The Sensology Workout – Waking Up the Senses* is a wonderful source of ideas.
www.amazon.co.uk/Sensology-Workout-Waking-Up-Senses/dp/0955900808

11

Facilitating sensory-being

Chapters 1–10 have equipped us with so much knowledge and so many ideas; we are ready to start sensory-being. In Chapter 11 Part A, we look at where we might share sensory-being with a Sensory Being. In Part B, we study how we can lead a Sensory Being into sensory-being, how we might go about facilitating sensory-being and how we will support a Sensory Being as sensory-being ends. In Part C, we will consider when we might share sensory-being. Finally, in Part D we will think about different themes for sensory-being, taking in options for using sensory-being to connect with memories or to form cultural connections, or as a way of spending time together, as well as considering how sensory-being could be utilised in an education context, looking at its merits for supporting learning skills, how we might differentiate it for different Sensory Being students and how we could use it to support different curriculum areas.

Part A: a space to be

After so much consideration of the stimuli we might use to inspire sensory-being, it is important we also consider the environment we will be in when sharing sensory-being and how this will influence the experience.

We have spent a lot of time considering objects to be foci for sensory-being, but a key to success in sensory-being is finding the right space to be in. This space does not have to be elaborate, but it must be valued.

Consider people who practice meditation: they may first have encountered meditation in a very special place, and then have tried to practice it at home. Perhaps they set up a dedicated space in their home; they probably ask people nearby not to interrupt them or plan to attempt to meditate at particular times when interruption is unlikely. From time to time, they may visit specialist locations to renew their motivation, but they may equally practice their techniques in busy spaces by creating their own small, peaceful focused space within the surrounding busyness. In creating a space for sensory-being, you are seeking to emulate these things.

Physically, you may want to create a space free from interruption with a plain background (in all senses, visually, auditorially, etc.) so as not to distract from the focus. In doing this, your main aim is not to create the Shangri-La perfect physical space, but to create a respected space. The physical aspects of the environment should support and not distract from the sensory-being activity, and they should also send a clear message to those around that this is a valued activity, not to be interrupted.

Of course, if it is just you and the individual you are supporting, then you are unlikely to need any physical setup beyond the immediate practicalities of getting comfortable, drawing a blind to protect you from unwanted glare and turning off the TV or radio. You may find outdoor environments particularly suitable for sensory-being. Some environments can provide both a space to be and objects for sensory-being in one – for example, a quiet spot in a garden where birdsong and bees buzzing provide the background track for watching the patterns of light and shade in the branches of a tree.

Simple bits of kit can help you to create a calm environment for sensory-being – for example, fabrics that you can drape over distracting objects or images; these could be bed sheets or towels. Upholstery base cloth is very cheap to buy and can provide a good matt black background. Small pop-up tents create instant sensory spaces. Cutting the bottom out of a tent can mean you can pop it over a person who uses a wheelchair whilst they are in their chair.

A small space helps people to feel secure. It could be a cupboard under the stairs, or something as simple as opening the wardrobe doors and throwing a blanket over the top of them to create a little den.

In busy spaces, it may be possible to use screens to create a quiet corner. Ideally, you would position the individual so that they have their back to the wall and screens obscure most of the rest of the environment. This is so they can have their space but not be surprised by people seeming to creep up on them. The padded screens commonly used as display boards are super at muffling sound.

A hula hoop hung so that its circle is parallel to the floor with fabric draped around it can make a good indoor tee-pee. You can buy all sorts of extraordinary shower curtains, including ones with fabulous prints – for example, of under-the-sea scenes or of starscapes – and, of course, plain ones. These are fun to thread onto a hoop to create small tents. If you are fortunate enough to have a bay window, drawing a curtain across the straight edge, dividing room from window, makes for a lovely, naturally lit space. Bendy tent poles and a little ingenuity or duct tape can be used to create a personalised tent around a wheelchair.

Numinous tent

This tent was created from four pieces of plastic plumber's pipe threaded through with string and suspended from a single point in the ceiling. The fabric making up the tent walls was bought off a roll at the local haberdashery in a length long enough to go around the four poles. Simple loops hang the fabric from the poles, creating a space big enough for several people to occupy at once. The open top allowed for subtle observation of the goings-on inside the tent.

I used this tent in my classroom a lot when I was a teacher in a school for students with severe and profound special needs. One of the most powerful things it enabled us to do was give the students an opportunity to be alone. For all of my students, this was a very rare thing. They lived incredibly supervised lives.

We saw significant behaviour changes inside the tent compared to outside. Children previously unaware of their peers reached out to embrace them. Children normally anxious calmed and stilled. It was such a simple thing: we just gave them a special space to be in, and the rest of what happened came from them.

If you are interested in further exploring the power of small environments, then it is worth finding out about Lilie Neilson's 'little rooms' and looking up Jean Ware's book: *Creating a Responsive Environment for People with Profound and Multiple Learning Difficulties*.

Hopefully these chapters have given you some ideas as to what to look for when hunting for stimuli for sensory-being. Remember, this will be a continual process – an ongoing and entertaining discussion between you and the person you support about what experiences are interesting. Now that you have a collection of sensory items, it is time to start thinking about the facilitation of sensory-being.

Part B: leading into being, facilitating being and moving on from being

We could have collected the best sensory resource to inspire sensory-being and found the perfect spot for sharing sensory-being, but if we then facilitate sensory-being with the subtlety of a bull in a china shop, then we ruin all of our careful preparation. In Part B, we spend time thinking about the delicacy of facilitating sensory-being.

Overview

The process of facilitating sensory-being is akin to blowing soap bubbles.

First, carefully, in a delicate, measured fashion, you blow the bubble, adjusting to subtle environmental factors as you do so: this is leading into sensory-being.

Next, you watch the beautiful colours slip and swirl around the surface of the bubble: this is facilitating sensory-being.

Finally, you observe the moment when the colours turn monochrome, the bubble film thins, becomes speckled and finally bursts. The bubble is gone: this is when you move on from sensory-being.

I am going to deal with these three stages in reverse order, taking first the moment when sensory-being ends.

Ending sensory-being

That point at which beauty ends, when the bubble pops, the sun sets, and the moment passes contains a gentle sadness. It is not a howling cry of pain, injustice or even loss, as we knew as we were in the moment that it was not infinite and would pass, but its absence is still felt, ever so slightly as a jolt, as a coming back to reality after something wonderful.

Choose an experience of your own of a moment like this: a sunset, a lover (who will return) waving goodbye, a concerto ending, a bouquet of flowers wilting, or simply a soap bubble popping. In that moment, if someone were to approach you and suggest a new activity, how would you want them to approach?

If they bounded up to you full of enthusiasm, this would demand effort from you. You would have to move between your slight low to their great high quickly enough not to miss the boat. If they were gloomy, you would not want to go with them, preferring to stay in your lesser sorrow than join their misery.

Someone stepping up and just announcing a new activity would be irksome. In their failing to acknowledge the moment just passed is an inherent disrespect for your experience, views and spirit.

But if someone approached you, and you felt in them a sense of respect for the moment passed, then you would be open to listening to their suggestion. Small rituals can help to convey this respect and give a routine to the moving on that makes it easier to do.

Moving on

When approaching someone to support them in moving on from sensory-being, we need to set our hearts to the same level as theirs. Remembering a similar personal moment should be enough to do this; come alongside them, join with them, and then once the connection is made, begin to move on.

Elements of ritual can be useful in conveying respect. Carefully packing an item away in a special box and putting a lid on, whilst in view (sensation) of the Sensory Being, demonstrates your appreciation for their experience.

A small song would work here. There is a free app called Ditty by Zya available on both Apple[1] and Android[2] that can be used to create and sing simple melodies. Uploading a simple message such as "It's time to stop sensory-being, let's put the box away" and choosing a free tune such as "Amazing Grace" for it to be sung to is ideal. Add in the person's name to make it personal.

Alternatively, you can adapt an old tune yourself. Nursery rhymes are often chosen, and they are super as they follow the engaging sing-song rhythm of motherese. If you are concerned about sounding babyish, steer away from popular ones and hunt out archaic ones forgotten from the modern litany. Another alternative is to source nursery rhymes from different cultural traditions.

Physical rituals can be especially nice, as touch is such a great communicator of 'with-ness.' These are easy to make up and all the better for being personalised. Here's an example.

> "Ahmad, Ahmad" – hands cupping Ahmad's shoulders and squeezing in a firm, reassuring manner to the beat of the name.
>
> "I'm here to say" – moving face and body close so he can sense you.
>
> "It's time to put these things away" – move hands from shoulders down the arms in an encircling stroke (assuming Ahmad was using his hands to take part in the activity).
>
> "Come what will and come what may, we'll get them out another day" – untangling item from Ahmad's fingers and packing it away safely.

Whatever you would naturally say to the person is probably the best. Adding a little rhythm, a little rhyme and some motions turns it into a ritual that will, in time, become familiar and comforting.

If you are working as part of a team, it is very important to ensure everyone understands that the ritual is *not* how you stop sensory-being, but how you demonstrate that you have noticed that sensory-being is over and that you are willing to be with the person as they move on. Without the pre-existing 'with-ness,' the ritual is meaningless and could even be hurtful or alienating, as it would serve only to highlight the inherent disconnect.

Facilitating sensory-being

In the main, it is expected that the individual will take part in sensory-being independently, so your role will be to unobtrusively withdraw your presence to allow their independence to take flight. Think about the soap bubble analogy: you will know from blowing bubbles (and if you do not have this knowledge immediately to hand in your brain, I insist you put this book down right away and go blow some bubbles to update your memory banks) that when a bubble is freshly blown, its surface is rich with colour and it is possible to slide objects in or out of the bubble without it popping. When the bubble is first blown, the wand is a part of the bubble's shape, but you allow the bubble to lift away from the wand, or you slide the wand away. In facilitating sensory-being, you are the wand and the breath, and the bubble is the other person's entrancement with the object.

In practical terms, this means an ongoing sequence of polite observances. You do not set someone up with a sensory-being object, move away and then yell instructions to someone else on the other side of the room. You do not set someone up with a sensory-being object and then create a kerfuffle with objects somewhere else in the room or start experimenting with a new crate of wonderfully distracting sensory resources.

There are plenty of things you can do as they enjoy sensory-being – just choose the tasks judiciously, and move around with consideration and respect for the bubble of their activity.

You are, of course, welcome to stay in the bubble. If you do this, try to keep the focus on the being, without transferring the attention solely to yourself. In doing this, you are showing respect for their engagement, learning and understanding. In a sense, they are saying "Wow, look at this thing I have discovered," and you are saying "Wow, yes, it is amazing." If, through your actions and expressions, you say, "Yes, that is amazing, now let me tell you about something amazing I know about" – although they may find what you offer fascinating – the underlying message is that you are better at discovering these amazing things than they are. However, if you let yourself be led by their absorption, then you are validating their discoveries and experiences, and in doing so boosting their confidence and self-esteem.

From bubbles to caves.

Here is a different analogy to elucidate sensory-being.

Imagine sensory-being like this:

> Two children (equals and innocents) in a fairytale land find a tunnel leading into an underground cave. Clasping hands, they walk together into the cave, perhaps one leading the other slightly. Inside the cave, they find a large, round, glittering stone. The first child lifts the stone to the light; the second child gasps and moves around the stone to see its brightness from a different angle. The second child reaches out, and the first child passes them the stone. The second child moves around, holding the stone up to the light absorbed by its beauty.

Contrast this with:

> Two children come across a tunnel leading into a cave. One child grabs the hand of the other child and drags them into the cave. Inside, they discover

a large, round, glittering stone. The first child declares "Oh wow," grabs the stone and hands it to the other child, who is instantly transfixed. Jealous of the attention the stone is getting, the first child talks loudly about how they discovered it and notes everything they know about it: how shiny it is, how it glitters in the light and that it is round.

When facilitating sensory-being, we are aiming to be like the first set of children, who approach the object and take part in its admiration as equals.

A third option would be:

The first child coaxes the second into the cave. Once the second child has seen the stone and the first child is confident of their amazement, the first child tiptoes away, allowing the second child to both discover and enjoy the stone on their own. The first child waits quietly at the mouth of the cave, ready to lead the second child out of the cave and back out to the sunlight.

Leading into sensory-being.

The two analogies I have used so far, of walking into a cave and of blowing soap bubbles, are a good starting point for understanding the culture required to lead into sensory-being. The cave analogy works well if you have a space designated for sensory-being, and the bubble analogy works well if you are going to provide opportunities for sensory-being in all sorts of locations. Most likely, you plan to do both.

Facilitation

How the object is offered is vital. We are honouring experience, inviting curiosity, allowing the person, the Sensory Being, to experience whatever they experience, trusting that this is okay and that whatever they experience is okay. How the facilitator communicates this will come from their own okay-ness with their own experience. The facilitator will communicate and support the intertwined strands of intention identified by Shapiro[1] as being involved in mindfulness practice: intention, attention and attitude.

Susannah Crump: MA, Post Graduate Certificate in Education (PGCE), Reg. British Association for Counselling & Psychotherapy (MBACP) (Snr. Accred.). Independent Counsellor; Teacher, Trainer and Supervisor of mindfulness-based approaches; member of the core training team for the Centre for Mindfulness Research and Practice at Bangor University. www.mindfulnessnorth-east.co.uk

[1] Dr Shapiro is a professional and clinical psychologist with an international reputation for expertise in mindfulness. www.drshaunashapiro.com

Leading into the cave.

No matter how beautiful and entrancing the object in the cave is, whether a person will want to stay in the cave and enjoy it will depend on how safe they felt as they were led into the cave, how safe they feel in the cave, and whether they feel free to leave the cave or whether they fear being trapped or abandoned for a long period of time in the cave.

If I were to take you to a cave with an extraordinary stone inside, how would you want our journey to progress?

For starters, if the cave just appeared around us in an unannounced fashion, you would be so shocked that you would instantly look for an escape. You would not care how pretty the inside of the cave was. The shock would block your ability to admire beauty. It would be dreadfully strange and disorientating to suddenly be plonked in a cave, yet for Sensory Beings who do not naturally understand or expect linear experiences, this kind of thing happens a lot: they just find themselves in places, having been brought to them in ways they cannot connect with.

Meaningful journeys

Sharon Cross recognised that making the physical journeys between activities meaningful would have a positive impact on a person's ability to engage and learn.[3]

Sharon worked with a student who was deaf-blind and had other cognitive impairments. She used four sensorially relevant stations along a route between the student's classroom and the multisensory room to engage and inform the student of her location.

On each journey to the multisensory room, the student was guided by the same verbal cues and given the opportunity to interact with four sensory experiences along the route.

Although this was a small-scale study of a single student, Sharon's results are in line with other studies that look at people experiencing sensory meaning in sequence – for example, studies focusing on sensory stories. The student showed increased engagement and understanding over repeated experiences of the route.

The three results tables below, taken from different stages in the study, tell an amazing story: first the student is unaware and takes time to respond to the stimuli, then the student becomes aware and responds. And in the last table, we see a student who takes almost no time to respond; they are already aware of the next stimulus before they get to it. In other words, they know where they are on their journey and where they are going, and they are actively engaged in being a part of the journey.

In Tables 11.1, 11.2 and 11.3, letters A, B, C and D correlate to particular stimuli along the route: a rough surface, a smooth surface, door handles that made noise and a tambourine.

Table 11.1 Week 1

Pauses in mobility route for landmarks to be explored	Seconds taken to initiate behaviour				Duration of behaviour			
	A	B	C	D	A	B	C	D
Moved head in the direction of wall or landmark	12	8	5	5	5	7	23	10
Lifted up arm/hand to explore wall or landmark	25	40	35	30	10	18	30	8
Vocalised	✓		✓	✓				
Smiled					✓			

Table 11.2 Week 6

Pauses in mobility route for landmarks to be explored	Seconds taken to initiate behaviour				Duration of behaviour			
	A	B	C	D	A	B	C	D
Moved head in the direction of wall or landmark	3	0	0	1	25	15	5	4
Lifted up arm/hand to explore wall or landmark	15	20	2	0	6	5	70	3
Vocalised			✓	✓				
Smiled	✓		✓					

Table 11.3 Week 10

Pauses in mobility route for landmarks to be explored	Seconds taken to initiate behaviour				Duration of behaviour			
	A	B	C	D	A	B	C	D
Moved head in the direction of wall or landmark	0	0	0	0	35	22	3	4
Lifted up arm/hand to explore wall or landmark	2	0	0	0	30	50	120	5
Vocalised	✓	✓	✓					
Smiled	✓	✓	✓					

Sharon says:

Deafblind children need to be actively engaged in order for learning to take place and repetitive and systematic routines are essential within this learning process.

In the discussion of her research, Sharon shares another interesting observation that reinforces insight we took in when looking at the findings from the perihand space research (see page 52 in Chapter 4). Sharon notes that often, the student would stop looking at a stimulus as she began to explore it with her hands. Individuals with a limited processing capacity may **need** to use their sensory systems in isolation in order to receive maximum information from them.

We must reflect on the impact this increased engagement with her journey had on the student and her experience of life at school. Knowing you are going to the multisensory room means you arrive ready for the experience, your sensory systems and brain warmed up and ready to go. Being the passive recipient of someone else's directing of your body in your wheelchair as you move towards an unknown location inspires a very different mental state. Making moments of transition meaningful has a powerful impact on a person's sense of agency and self-worth, as well as on their ability to engage with the activity.

If the cave did not just appear, but was there before us and I pushed you in, then it could go either way, and which way it went would depend on your personality. If I take your hand and tell you about a wonderful cave whilst walking towards it, making sure you are happy, and once inside I step back gently to let you have the joy of discovery for yourself, that would be an experience of togetherness and wonder.

Sensory tours

Sensory tours are a way to create a meaningful connection with a place for Sensory Beings. Over the past few years, I have created several tours on behalf of various heritage settings within the UK.

At Hampton Court Palace, I worked with the team in charge of Sensory Palaces, a health and well-being programme for people living with dementia and their carers, to create a sensory tour of the King's State Apartments. We chose ten points of sensory and historic interest from around the apartments and wove them together to create a historical narrative resourced with experiences from within the rooms, and also experiences brought in especially for the tour. The Hampton Court Palace staff were marvellous and gave me a perfumist to work with who created the smell of Georgian sweat to be used on the tour: what a smell!

At the London Transport Museum, I worked with the engagement and inclusion team to create a sensory tour that took experiencers on a journey through the history of transport in London. The challenge of creating this tour was very different to other tours I have written. The London Transport Museum is a very stimulating environment. In creating the tour, we had to work to find ways to block out the multitude of background experiences in order to allow experiencers to focus on the sensory meaning before them.

Creating sensory tours is a way of inviting Sensory Beings to explore a place in a way that is relevant to them. Sensory tours can also be used to enable people to brave a new experience: by sharing the tours in advance of a visit, people can prepare themselves for what to expect when they get there. Sensory tours can be used to support people to remember a visit. By sharing the tours after the visit, we help people to connect with their memories of visiting that place.

In real-world terms, what does all of this mean?

It means that the activity of sensory-being begins for the facilitator prior to the arrival in the space for being. It is about attitude, and being attuned to the person you are travelling with. If the person you are leading into sensory-being has something they want to express, it is about attending to that first, before expecting them to follow the route you have planned.

If you are going to be going on a physical journey into sensory-being – for example, from a classroom to a multisensory room – it is about finding a way to tell the person you are travelling with where you are going and whereabouts in that journey you are.

Objects of reference

Objects of reference are one way of sharing information about activities with a Sensory Being. An object of reference is an object that holds meaning for the Sensory Being about the activity it refers to. So, for example, if a Sensory Being is going to have a bath, the object might be the flannel that will be a part of the bathing activity.

It is important when choosing objects of reference that we choose objects that hold meaning for the Sensory Being, not objects we see as being representative of an activity. For example, we might associate a purse with shopping, as this is something we handle when shopping. However, the Sensory Being's experience of shopping is different to ours. Shopping to them might be the electric strip lighting used in the supermarket, or the whirring of the air conditioning units, or the coldness of the freezer aisle, etc. What object is actually a part of their supermarket experience? Keith Park, who contributed the box below, advises that the best objects of reference are a meaningful part of the experience they cue in; are objects that the Sensory Being finds motivating; and relate to an experience that the Sensory Being has frequently.

Objects of reference

One of the most celebrated paintings of the Belgium surrealist Magritte is of an apple, underneath which appear the words 'Ceci n'est pas une pomme' (This is not an apple). Because of course, it is the picture of an apple, not the apple itself. You can't eat it.

Objects of reference are usually understood to refer to the use of an object as a reference to a particular object, person or activity. A cup for drink, a fork for dinner, and so on.

It all sounds so straightforward. But it is often assumed that a person can already understand that an object can 'stand for' or represent something completely separate. "Let's use a car key on a piece of card for 'going in a car.' " Why? The key is on a card and isn't used in the activity.

Objects of reference are a great resource with a wonderful potential, but it begs the bigger question: how do we all learn that words, signs, symbols and objects of reference refer to things that they themselves are not? This is not an apple!

Keith Park: author of *Objects of Reference: Promoting Early Symbolic Communication*, published in 2002 (3rd edition) by The Royal National Institute for the Blind. Available on Amazon: http://ow.ly/dbgP306dS03

We need to be careful to remember our Linguist Being bias. Once we realise how brilliantly objects of reference can work to aid a Sensory Being's understanding, it is all too easy to quickly begin to think of them as a language in themselves – to think that if we could just find objects to reference everything, then we would be able to build a dialogue between us and the Sensory Being. Sadly, having zillions of objects of reference can destroy the meaning of the few good ones in the mix. Choose a few relevant objects that can be frequently used and all will be well.

Part C: when we will share sensory-being

We have considered what we will use to inspire sensory-being, we have considered where we will share sensory-being and we have considered how we will facilitate sensory-being. In Part C, we will consider when we will share sensory-being. With all these things taken into account, we will look at a step-by-step summary of how we will share sensory-being.

When will we blow these bubbles of sensory-being?

Here is a situation you may have seen: in a busy environment, a Sensory Being has a moment where they are going to be left to occupy themselves whilst those around them get on with another task, such as preparing medication. The person supporting this individual reaches for a couple of sensory toys and offers them to the individual, asking which they want. Receiving no clear response, the person makes a decision and places one of the toys into the individual's grasp. They then put the other toy away and get on with what they were going to do.

Perhaps the person explores the object, perhaps they drop it, disinterested. Perhaps they do not realise they have it and it remains unexplored within their grasp.

The moment described is an ideal sensory-being opportunity. To utilise this moment for sensory-being will take a little longer than just handing over a random object, but this effort is more than rewarded by how much more meaningful the moment becomes when sensory-being is enabled.

I am not being critical of the imagined facilitator in the moment described above. In offering the individual an object to explore, they have done something very important: they have recognised that the Sensory Being's moment-to-moment experience of life continues when they step away.

A different situation is where Linguistic Beings do not recognise that each moment is of equal importance for Sensory Beings. For example, a Linguistic Being will have a fabulous multisensory activity planned. It just takes a bit of setting up. The Sensory Beings in their care are parked around the edge of the room as the activity is set up. They then get to take part in the activity, before being parked again, as it is packed away. Perhaps they remain parked whilst the next activity is set up. At the end of the day, the Linguistic Being looks back in their memory and sees a day full of exciting activities. Their memory skips over the transitional moments. But the Sensory Beings have experienced a day punctuated by periods of disorientation and aloneness. Some of these periods may have caused them to shut down their sensory systems, to begin to pay attention inwards rather than outwards, to become less capable of being active and engaged.

Linguistic Beings can be under enormous pressure from outside influences – for example, staff shortages – and internal ones – for example, a desire to create a really brilliant session for the Sensory Beings in their care. There is always a balance to be struck between what is ideal and what is practical. Sometimes just remembering that the Sensory Beings in your care do not need a session to have a multitude of elaborate resources or hours of planning behind it can be a help to everyone involved. Just a few simple items that they enjoy and your presence and company can be as rewarding for them as the most fabulously constructed multisensory performance. Remember also that the pressure does not come from them. You are their friend. They would not want you to feel stressed because of them. They do not want you missing your breaks in order to set up a session for them. They would probably rather just sit with you and share a chat.

Each and every moment is important to a Sensory Being. The person who hands over the sensory object before leaving recognises the continuous experience of the Sensory Being. The person who takes the time to present an opportunity for sensory-being before leaving honours that continuous experience.

Mindful transitions

When I am teaching mindfulness practices I encourage my students to maintain their attention to the present during transitions between activities. I invite them to bring their attention to those moments in which we move from one place to another: how is it to feel the sensation of pressure on my side as I lever myself to sitting up; on my knees as I move to kneeling; how does the chair feel as I sit down? Activities may begin and end, but moments are continuous and our presentness in them can be too.

Susannah Crump: MA, Teacher, trainer and supervisor of mindfulness-based approaches; Member of the core training team for the Centre for Mindfulness Research and Practice at Bangor University. www.mindfulnessnorth-east.co.uk

Creating a bubble around a moment

If we were the facilitator who needed to step away for a moment to deal with a task, instead of just handing over a sensory object, how could we blow a bubble of sensory-being around that moment?

Step one.
Preparation: have to hand items that are likely to inspire sensory-being.
Step two.
Take a friendly, non-judgemental interest in the sensory experiences you are having in the present moment. These might be linked to the object you plan to share with the Sensory Being you are supporting, or they might be experiences from the wider environment. Whatever they are, just notice them and accept them as they are. As you centre yourself in this way so you will become more in sync with the Sensory Being you are supporting.

How we are affects how those around us are

Here, Special Yoga practitioner Jo Manuel talks about the children who attend special schools with whom she works, but her words apply to us all.

Children with special needs are like sponges. . .they absorb everything: our energy, our emotions. It is said so often in the spiritual world that everything begins with a thought, and then the thought becomes speech and then the speech becomes actions. So our thoughts matter. Our state matters. It is as if these children can read our thoughts. Children don't learn from what we say, they learn from who we are and how we manage our emotional states. So when we are calm, organised, open hearted and compassionate we are able to see the child/children as they truly are – beyond whatever behaviours are presenting themselves. In this place we are able to see the true nature of the children and the child is honoured, respected, trusted, loved and held. When we are reactive we will only be able to see the behaviours and not the true child because we are not sitting in our true nature. In our own true nature we slow down and can meet the child where they are. And then we can enter their world and bring them to where we can help support their potential.

Jo Manuel: Founder of the Special Yoga Foundation CIO. http://specialyoga.org.uk; Jo has more than 25 years of experience working with young people with special educational needs and disabilities.

Step three.

Once you have connected with your own experience, and steadied your internal monologue and whirlwind of emotions, approach the person and connect with them. You may signal your presence through any of the sensory systems. If you know the person well, you may choose to signal your presence through the sensory system they process best.

Step four.

Wait for a connection to be formed. Understand that this may take some time; you may be waiting minutes, not seconds. Remember that there are two equal parts to this process, and your announcing of your presence is only half of the whole event.

There is a subtlety to this, as the point of the exercise is not to draw attention to yourself but simply to offer that sense of accompaniment. You are presenting yourself as a companion, not as entertainment. You are offering 'with-ness' like the children walking into the cave.

Step five.

Present the sensory-being object. Remain a while as the individual focuses in on the object. Involving yourself in the co-exploration of the object with the individual can support them in attuning their awareness to it.

Imagine you are showing someone, who has never seen it before, the ripple a pebble makes when dropped into a still pond. You might take them close to the pond, throw a pebble or two yourself, taking time between your throws to allow them to notice the ripples, and then help them to locate and throw a pebble, before leaving them to delight in the patterns they are creating.

In beginning sensory-being, you can gently, slowly, show the person you are supporting how to hold and manipulate the object. You might support them in examining it and discovering its attributes. Always allow the person you are supporting to have the agency and power in these co-explorations. As far as possible, be led by them; in this way, the lead explorer role can slip from your shoulders to theirs, and once they are fully in control, you can step back and slip away for a brief while. Some people may independently focus on sensory-being for many minutes; for others, it may be that you are measuring independence in seconds.

Seconds are precious

If someone is only able to engage in sensory-being for a few seconds, this does not mean sensory-being is not right for them. If anything, it makes it all the more precious, as they are someone who is unlikely to experience opportunities for independence in their day-to-day lives. The rarity of these few seconds of independence makes them extra precious.

As with leading out of being, adding an element of ritual and routine can be a good route into being. This can be a simple song or sequence of actions, as described in leading out of being, or something a little more elaborate, like a sensory story.

Sensory stories

Sensory stories are concise texts in which each line of the text is accompanied by a sensory experience chosen for its relevance to the text and for its sensory qualities. They are fabulous resources. I was so enamoured by sensory stories that I wrote a whole book about them which curious readers may want to look up: sensory stories for children and teens (and adults).[4] Sensory stories can be used as a route into sensory-being.

When creating a sensory story, to lead into sensory-being, choosing the last stimulus in the story is of supreme importance. It needs to be a stimulus that continues, so something like a horn that sounds and stops, or a taste that is eaten and is gone would be no good. Sounds and tastes can be used, but you would be looking for something like a lolly that could be enjoyed for a long time or a piece of music that would play and play.

Sensory stories for people with dementia

I supported Coralie Oddy in creating a sensory story for individuals with dementia. Here Coralie describes her experience of sharing the story. The story is available to purchase from http:jo.element42.org/sensory-stories.

I shared a sensory story I had written called 'Wildlife in the City' in a gardening and reminiscence group for people living with dementia. As moving to a new location can be a disorienting experience for a person with dementia, I envisaged the story as a way of cueing group members into where they were and what was about to happen. I wanted the story to help the group realise "Here I am. It must be time for gardening. I'm ready to do that."

This worked well – the sensory objects became familiar to the members of the group, and they would sit down anticipating the story. The sensory experiences – such as the scent of peppermint or the sound of the rain – were also great conversation starters and triggers for memories. But what was really interesting was the sense of calm focus each retelling of the story seemed to give the group.

"Wildlife in the City" ends with the sound of birdsong. The first time I told the story, I played the birdsong for as long as the whole group seemed to be attending to and enjoying the sound – about ten seconds. After a few retellings, this increased to well over a minute. The group seemed to be developing their capacity for quiet reflection. For a short time, they were in a relaxed but attentive frame of mind – so different from the agitated or passive states people with advanced dementia can often inhabit. Engaging their senses within a familiar sequence supported them in finding a sense of peace.

Coralie Oddy: Speech and Language Therapist, Sensory Story Author and Founder of ReminiSense. https://remini-sense.com

Part D: themes for sensory-being

Sensory-being is a wonderful activity in and of its own right, but for one reason or another, you may be interested in theming sensory-being around particular goals or topics. In Part D, we look at how sensory-being can be used as a tool for facilitating cultural connection, connecting with memories and being together.

Cultural connection

Many heritage settings seek to find ways to fully include members of the public who may not be able to access their exhibits through the traditional means of reading text and viewing objects. Creating cultural connection through sensory-being will be ideal for these settings and also for settings significant to communities – for example, faith settings.

In these settings, you are looking to discover an object from the setting that has the sensory properties required for sensory-being, or to create a sensory object that represents the setting.

Here is an example from my local area.

Truro Cathedral

Truro Cathedral has a chalice made from the melted-down gold of many parishioners' donated rings and set with the gemstones from those rings. It is an extraordinary object that holds within itself so many stories. It also glitters and sparkles and is heavy and cold, making it a wonderful object for sensory-being. A person holding the chalice touches those stories, experiences the meaning held within it in a sensory way. It is a unique experience that belongs to the Cathedral alone. In holding the chalice, a Sensory Being connects to the Cathedral in a manner that is meaningful to them. Linguistic Beings must remember that connection is not something experienced through language alone.

Memory

An object from a place, a person or a time can give us a sensory connection to memory. Anyone who has lost a loved one will know how powerfully objects can connect us to memories: old clothes, items the person treasured, jewellery, locks of hair.

During the time that I was writing this book, my Grandmother passed away. Some people leave surprisingly big holes in our lives, and although she lived far away, and I saw her rarely, the hole she left was huge. One of the many things she loved to do in life was watch the birds in her garden. My life has always been too busy to watch the birds. But now I have a bird feeder set up outside the living room window, and I enjoy simply sitting and watching the birds. It is my own time of sensory-being, and the connection that I feel with my Grandmother in doing this is ongoing.

Equal Justice Initiative's Community Remembrance Project

The Equal Justice Initiative's Community Remembrance Project recognises and remembers the thousands of African Americans who have been the victims of racially motivated lynching. The Project collects soil from the sites of lynchings and keeps the soil in jars as a memorial. They find that the physical presence of the soil brings meaning to their memorial beyond that which words can express alone.

Lawyer and Founder of the Equal Justice Initiative, Bryan Stevenson, talked about the jars of different coloured soil, each with a name of a victim upon it, on Radio 4's documentary The Green Book, broadcast on the 29th of November 2016.He said:

"You smell that scent, that's the dirt. It's the scent of the soil, and for us it is important that there be something visible and tangible that you can touch and feel and smell that

connects you to this history of lynching and suffering. There's sweat in the soil, it's the sweat of the enslaved people, there are tears in the soil, it's the anguish of people who were menaced and threatened. There is blood in the soil, it's the blood of the broken bodies of people who were lynched and maimed."

http://eji.org/community-remembrance-project

Being together

Finding activities where you can share enjoyment of sensory-being with a Sensory Being can be nourishing and bonding. You need an activity that you find absorbing which also holds absorbing sensory properties for the person with whom you hope to share the activity. You may need to loosen your idea of what the activity is for you. This can be a good practice in extending your own mindfulness; for example, if you choose a colouring activity, you may at first see your goal as colouring something perfectly within the lines, but when your companion becomes engaged in your movements and reaches out for the colour, your plans of perfection need adapting. If you can allow the change to happen and accept it as part of the process, you will find beauty in the new joint creation. Practicing this acceptance can help you build your capacity to accept the changing circumstances of life.

Here are a few activities that could work as joint sensory-being activities:

Colouring in: Try choosing concentric circles or geometric patterns, and choose bright contrasting colours. Be sure to have your paper at the right distance from the person you are sharing the activity with for them to be able to enjoy the changing visuals.

Cooking: Be prepared for your recipe to take a while. Slow yourself down on purpose and notice the aspects of cooking you might not notice alone: the differing smells, textures and how things look as your baking progresses. Find ways to bring the experience near to the person you are supporting – for example, can you place the bowl on their lap? Can they handle the ingredients? Or ways to add sensory interest to the processes: can you chop in a heartbeat rhythm?

Knitting: Sit close, enable the Sensory Being to hold the ball of wool as it gradually unwinds, and listen to the steady clicking of your needles.

Finger knitting: Choose a lovely textured, chunky, brightly coloured wool and knit it carefully around the fingers of the Sensory Being. Practice, and collaboration will grow.

Arm knitting: Using one arm each as needles, knit together.

Nature watching: Find a space in nature and be together. Allow the Sensory Being to take the lead in this one; your role is to take the time to notice what they notice.

Singing: Sing your heart out. Your companion can enjoy the music or join in with their vocalisations or movements.

Breathing and being: Sit together and just pause for a moment. Pay attention to your own breath and to the breath of your partner. And allow everything else to be as it is.

Curriculum

In schools, sensory-being may need to be justified as part of the curriculum. We could argue that there is a need for down time, in order for our brains to recharge and be ready to learn, but justifying sensory-being as a part of the curriculum in this way is self-defeating as it frames it from the outset as something outside of the curriculum and does not recognise the potential for learning within it.

Sensory-being for Sensory Beings, in an education context, is a wonderful, independent learning activity. The next section of this chapter presents examples of sensory-being explained in terms of different curriculum contexts, but first we are going to look at the education significance of the independence of sensory-being.

Independent learning

Learning independently is an incredibly precious thing, no matter what we learn. Young children, given free time, often focus in on one small aspect of an activity, observing it intently – for example, a child poking in the sand with a stick, or the child in a playground who chooses to go on one piece of equipment repeatedly. They create their own moments of sensory learning. These pauses for focused observation yield points of rich, vivid knowledge. The relevance of these knowledge points is not immediately obvious when considered individually, but taken together, they form a network of understanding: little sign posts by which the collector of these points may navigate the world.

Remember the starscape of random points of knowledge we discussed in Chapter 2? It is the freedom, the independence, of these moments of sensory discovery that creates such intense points of knowledge. Being told to closely observe something will never yield the same quality of knowledge. The strength of knowledge obtained through sensory-being is the first benefit of its independence.

The second benefit of the independence of sensory-being is to the person, not the mind, and is paid out in self-esteem, self-worth and the combating of learned helplessness. However small, being able to do something *on your own* leads to a sense of 'I can'; this is especially valuable to people who need a lot of support.

Sensory learning across the curriculum

With all subjects, it helps to be philosophical when considering the place of sensory-being within the curriculum: we must boil the topic of study down to its essence and understand that learning about this essence is fundamental for understanding the topic.

The requirement to understand the essence of a topic in order to effectively learn is true for everyone. I was once invited to support a young man at secondary school who was having trouble with his maths. My role was to investigate what was causing his problems. After a few days of exploration, I discovered that, although this young man was able to recall the answers to his times tables and manipulate simple equations, he had no underlying concept of number. To him, maths was about numbers: you put numbers in, you got numbers out. In his mind, all these numbers were the same; he had no sense of how much a number was. When his calculations produced what to me seemed like a fantastically unlikely answer, he just saw a number, as plausible to him as any other. A concept of number is fundamental to mathematical understanding at every level. We develop our concept of number in early sensory explorations as we experience things that are singular and things that are many.

When we talk about the boiled-down essence of a subject being the heart of a curriculum-based sensory-being object, we are not suggesting that the Sensory Being we offer this experience to is taking part in some lesser aspect of the subject. It is not tokenistic, not a subject 'lite' or a play version of a real thing. We are attempting to offer the fundamentals, the distilled, highly concentrated, cold, hard foundations of a subject.

Play

*Play drives an innate desire for learning, mastery, meaning-making, and enjoyment. It helps us to develop thinking and language skills, through becoming completely engrossed in play we learn co-ordination and body control skills. When at play we are completely engaged; this is important because it triggers the reward aspect in the Hippocampus, which is the brain's key structure for memory and learning. **Play is a powerful tool that enables much deeper learning to happen.***

For educators and carers choosing the right sensory experience can be a way of enabling a person to access effective play. When we have the privilege of joining in with that play we also access something very precious in those magic moments, where an imaginative spark is understood and shared by both parties on a sensory level.

Ruth Churchill Dower: Director, Earlyarts. http://earlyarts.co.uk

Subject areas

For each subject below, I have provided a distilled definition of the area of study, together with examples of how sensory-being might provide an opportunity for independent study of the subject. You are free to create your own definitions and use them to spark ideas for sensory connections to the subject.

Art

Art is expressive engagement with shape, colour and texture.

Any object that offers the opportunity for texture shape and colour to be encountered offers Sensory Beings the opportunity to engage with art.

The structured sensory art project

The structured sensory art project was set up to enable people with profound and multiple learning disabilities to independently create works of art. It recognised that when creation is independent, the sensory activity of engaging with shape, colour and texture not only entertains and engages, but benefits a person's sense of self and personal agency.

The artists involved in the project were offered responsive painting rigs to paint with and had their painting facilitated in a way designed to awaken and alert them to the activity and allow them maximum agency within it.

You can view videos of the studio, rigs and artists, and the tour of their exhibition, Uninhibited, at http://jo.element42.org/the-structured-sensory-art-project

Having a disability may limit you physically and mentally, but it does not limit your capacity for creativity.

Maths

Maths is an appreciation of quantity and sequence.

Maths can include sensory-being experiences of single objects and multiple objects, and experiences of sequence – for example, scales in music or patterns; experiences of capacity, things being full or empty.

Literacy and Languages (our own or those of others)

Literacy is about conveying meaning, and language is a part of that.

Any exchange counts. There is meaning in all the sensory world, and there is communication when we hand a sensory item to a Sensory Being and when they respond to it.

Reading

Offer sensory-being objects hidden in some way – for example, beneath a blanket, in a peg bag or in a box. Always keep the same item in the same concealment. Offer the Sensory Being multiple opportunities to experience the items. When a Sensory Being recognises from the box that a favourite object will be inside, they are 'reading' the lid of the box – for example, knowing that inside the box with the red lid will be their favourite red toy.

Writing

Any sensory-being object that involves mark-making counts as writing, as when we write we translate our thoughts into marks. When a Sensory Being interacts with an object, they are physically manifesting their thoughts, and if this results in a mark of any kind, then they have a written record of their expression. Marks do not have to be in ink or paint; they can be in sand or sequins, they do not have to be on paper, they can be talcum powder on the skin, or scratches in wax.

Speaking and listening

Speaking is conveying meaning through sound, and listening is taking meaning onboard through our auditory systems. Sensory-being objects that offer the person experiencing them to make or cause noise are ideal, and if these are shared with a facilitator who is able to support the turn-taking nature of communication, then a lovely conversation can ensue.

Science

Science is the systematic questioning and exploring of the world.

Science can include repeated experiences of light/dark, heavy/light, growth/decay, wet/dry, hot/cold, push/pull, wood/metal/plastic.

Technology

Technology is about understanding how things work.

Getting involved in the creation of a sensory-being box is a part of understanding how it works, even if that is simply an understanding that glue is sticky!

Technology can include discovering simple cause-and-effect situations – for example, pulling a string rings a bell, pressing a button makes a noise.

Create a being-box with a clasp to be studied or handle that can be used by a Sensory Being to open the box.

Geography

Geography is an understanding of place.

Create sensory-being experiences inspired by sensory experiences particular to a place – for example, foods, artworks. (See cultural connection, page 160).

Creating a sensory experience out of an aspect of a place can highlight the sensory attributes of a place – for example, the homemade crystal kaleidoscope online in Chapter 10 could be used to look at a place.

History

History is knowledge of the past.

History is immediately created moment to moment, so historical sensory-being can begin with exploring an item from earlier in today, or from yesterday. You can explore items from a person's personal history – for example, toys or clothing from when they were younger. You can explore objects of historical significant, like Truro Cathedral's chalice (page 161).

PSHE – Personal Social Health Education

One of the biggest contributions sensory-being of any kind can add to the study of PSHE for a Sensory Being is the opportunity to promote their mental health through experiences of independence.

Being together (page 162) is a wonderful, low-pressure way to learn social skills, such as collaboration.

Sensory objects could be chosen that relate to aspects of personal care – for example, toothbrushes, flannels, etc. The opportunity to explore these in one's own time will make having them used on you less alarming and more understood.

Physical education

Physical education is the process of developing and honing physical skills.

Sensory-being will necessarily entail the honing of physical skills. Remember that seeing involves moving the muscles in the eyes, smelling involves controlling muscles that draw air into our bodies, and so on. (See Parallel London box on pages 33–34 in Chapter 2.)

Differentiating sensory-being for different learners

You can expect a range of abilities and learning styles from students for whom sensory-being is an appropriate form of learning, and you can differentiate sensory-being according to these differences.

- Some students may be particularly motivated by social contact and find the independence of sensory-being challenging.

Try finding experiences that offer some social feedback – for example, mirrors where one may socialise with oneself, or sound experiences that offer voices or other aspects of social interaction.

You will, of course, be offering these students lots of time to socialise with you and with peers. Sensory-being is just one activity in their sphere of experience.

- Some students may be willing to engage, seemingly indiscriminately, with any object, but seem to get fed up quickly.

Remember, interest in an object can trigger rejection (see Chapter 7). Try supporting these students in a physical way to maintain their attention on one object – for example, by offering them an experience attached to a pendulum so that when they throw it away, it goes away for a little while but then returns to be re-explored. Or place an item to be explored in the foot of a sock or pair of tights, and pull the tights over the arm of the Sensory Being so they can feel the object in the foot.

Remember also that jumping your attention from one experience to the next is a natural part of acquiring knowledge (see the explore and connect section of Chapter 2). You may be able to facilitate this shifting attention within a tray of activities; try offering a range of experiences to be explored at will.

- Some students may be willing to engage with any object and are able to sustain their attention for a relatively long period of time.

Find ways to increase the complexity of experience for these students. For example, by pointing a beam of light onto a shiny sensory-being object so that, as well as enjoying the shininess of the object, the student exploring it can also notice the beam of light and how it is there when they move the object one way, but not when they move it another. Or increase the complexity of the object – for example, by presenting the student with a sensory-being box that can be opened or closed so that in their explorations, they discover how to open and close the box and get different experiences depending on whether the box is open or closed. The ladybird from Plush Art Lab is a super example of an experience that offers potential for increasing complexity.

A sensory ladybird

The ladybird is red; it has areas of high-contrast, bold block colours; it has a face; it is heavy to hold; and it ticks so many boxes for early developmental sensory experiences.

Exploring it, you discover it makes a noise if you shake it, and it squeaks if you pinch its head. Each of its legs is filled with a different material. The legs can be folded inside pockets on its underside.

The wings are secured by Velcro tabs. When these are undone, more layers are revealed below with lots of other textures and visuals to explore. It is a gorgeous object that can be explored at a very basic level, but can also be investigated in a much more sophisticated manner.

The ladybird was kindly made for and donated to the Sensory-being project by Plush Art Lab, who have generously provided instructions as to how it was made publically on their website at: www.plushartlab.com/blog/making-of-the-sensory-plush-ladybug

- Some students may feel particularly vulnerable when not closely supported, and although not motivated primarily by the social contact, their ability to engage when alone will be impaired by this lack of confidence.

Support these students by staying physically close as they engage in sensory-being, and over time, gradually make your presence less and less felt – for example, by consciously making an effort to be quiet and still, fading yourself out until they are able to maintain short periods of focus without feeling that you are near. It is valuable for them to have experiences of feeling safe when alone, so that when they experience being alone for short periods of time in the future, they are not distressed.

Mindful facilitation

Mindfulness is a radical way of relating to our experience. It has no goal other than to be present. It involves paying attention to the moment in a fundamentally kind, accepting and playfully curious way. We allow the experience we are having to be. We allow the people in that experience with us to be. Sensory Beings can embody this with their intense curiosity and wonder.

Babies are a good example of how important the facilitator role can be for Sensory Beings, as without their parent or protector present a baby will not engage with the world with joyful wonder but will instead become distressed. The difference is not one of environment or sensory stimulus; it is the presence or absence of that sense of security.

Mindfulness involves allowing the flow of pleasant, unpleasant and neutral experiences to occur naturally without us trying to hold onto or rush particular experiences. Sensory Beings are great at allowing experience to be fluid: their moods change from content to miserable and back again so quickly as they react to experience as it flows. Being around people who are so great at allowing experience to flow and paying attention to these abilities in them is a good way for us to learn to let things flow a bit more.

Susannah Crump: MA, Teacher, trainer and supervisor of mindfulness-based approaches; Member of the core training team for the Centre for Mindfulness Research and Practice at Bangor University. www.mindfulnessnorth-east.co.uk

Notes

1   https://itunes.apple.com/gb/app/ditty-by-zya/id957529556?mt=8
2   https://play.google.com/store/apps/details?id=com.zya.ditty&hl=en_GB
3   Sharon Cross is a Special Advisory Teacher supporting children who are deaf-blind in mainstream and special school settings; she is also a Member of Lancashire Council's SEND Traded Team. See Cross, S. (2015) Special study: Enhancing mobility and orientation for children with multi-sensory impairments: A case study of an MSI learner who uses a wheelchair. Dissertation submission for the University of Birmingham.
4   Grace, J. (2014) *Sensory Stories for Children and Teens with Special Educational Needs.* Jessica Kingsley Publishers, available online at: http://ow.ly/AvzT302khPV

12

Conclusion

Traditionally books end with words of conclusion from their author. Not this book. The team of Sensory Being Consultants were by far and away the most important influence not only on the writing of this book, but on the wider reaching Sensory-being project. The final expressed meaning in these pages should be theirs.

It is hard to capture all of the meaning they conveyed so eloquently in our interactions. Nothing beats being there in the moment, but in these of photos from our conversations, I believe you will perceive a clear message.

You are the important part of this process for us.

When you support us in feeling safe, we feel confident exploring with you and on our own.

We rely on you to bring us the experiences we explore.

You are the difference.

We enjoy being with you.

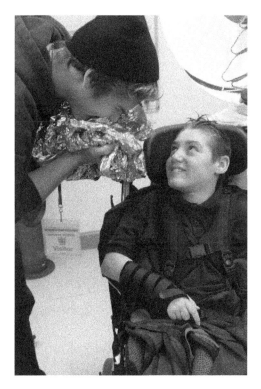

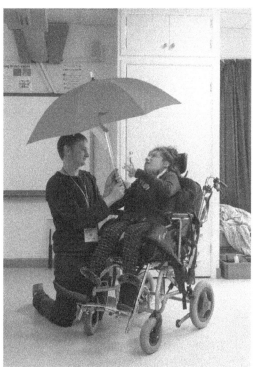

We love these experiences.

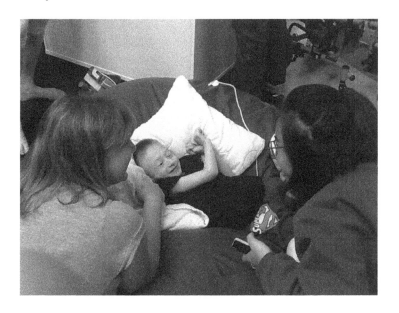

Appendix

Photocopy these pages and ask everyone who knows the Sensory Being you are supporting to have a go at filling out a copy. Share and compare your insights, and reflect on what you have picked up on. Complete the portrait again at a later date: what has changed?

You do not have to use the whole page. Simply choosing a few questions about each sense and asking them of people regularly will mean you will encourage those who form a network around a Sensory Being to become habitual sensory detectives, noticing and picking up on sensory preferences and abilities. This increased awareness will help everyone to find experiences that connect and engage.

A visual portrait of _____(name of Sensory Being) by_____ (name of person sharing their insight) on_____(date the portrait was written)

Use your sight to evaluate my visual experience of the world. On a day-to-day basis, what visual experiences are on offer to me? Think of my visual journey through the day, what do I see?

What do I look at? Do you notice me looking at particular things? What are these things? Do they have anything in common? Where are they? Is there a connection between how they are presented?

Where in my environment are the things I see best? Do I need things to be close to me, further away from me? To a particular side of me? Do I need to be able to wear glasses to see better?

Am I interested in brightly coloured objects?

Do I show interest in lights?

Are my eyes drawn to objects that wiggle or jiggle a little?

Do my eyes follow objects that move across my visual field?

Can I look at objects in a cluttered visual environment, or do I need a relatively plain background behind an object before I focus on it?

What are my favourite things to look at? Do I recognise anything? What makes me happy when I see it?

Are there any safety concerns that it is important people are aware of with regards to the visual stimuli I get to experience?

An olfactory account of _____(name of Sensory Being) by _____ (name of person filling in the page) on _____(date observations were made).

What do you know about my early smellscape? What smells did I encounter when I was very young?

Do I like the smell of hot sweet things?

What smells do you notice me noticing?

Do I respond to smells I make myself?

Do I have a comfort blanket or toy? What does that smell like?

Am I comforted by the smell of your clothing?

Can you think of a few places I visit regularly? What smells are distinct to these places?

What do the products that are used around me smell like, e.g. hand soap, laundry detergent, etc.?

Do I have a favourite smell?

Remember, if you do not know the answer to a question, do not worry – we can find it out together later. If you try to answer it by asking me to smell lots of different smells one after another, I might not be able to help you, as it is likely my nose will get tired after the first two.

Are there any safety concerns that it is important people are aware of with regards to the olfactory stimuli I get to experience?

A soundscape of _____(name of Sensory Being) by _____(name of person filling in the page) on _____(date observations were made).

My soundscapes:

What were the sounds around me when I was very little? What songs would have been on the radio? Would the washing machine have been on? Did we live somewhere where the wind rattled the windows, or cars drove by in the night?

What are the sounds around me in the settings you know me in?

Whose voices do I hear regularly? Do they have particular phrases they say?

How do I join in with conversations? Do I make my own noises, or do I show you I am joining in in other ways?

What are my favourite sounds? Do I have a particular type of sound I enjoy most, e.g. people's voices, or jangly noises, loud noises, deep rumbly noises, etc.?

What sounds do I make? What sounds do I hear from around myself; does my tummy rumble, do my clothes rustle?

What sort of soundscape do I live in at home? Is it muffled, with lots of soft furnishings and drapes, etc.? Or sharper, with hard flooring and reflective surfaces? How do I respond to contrasting soundscapes?

Are there any sounds that frighten me?

Are there sounds that I enjoy making that aren't vocalisations, e.g. ringing bells, or bashing objects against one another?

What are my favourite songs?

Are there any safety concerns that it is important people are aware of with regards to the auditory stimuli I get to experience?

The tastes of _____(name of Sensory Being) by _____ (name of person filling in the page) on _____(date observations were made).

What did my first food taste and smell like? Was it baby food? Milk? Did I have a gastrostomy? What was I fed through it?

What are my favourite foods? Is there a particular type of food I like the best, e.g. sweet, salty?

Are there any foods I do not like?

What foods do I get to smell regularly? Do I smell food cooking at dinner or at lunch time? What does it smell like?

What foods do I get to touch regularly? Do my fingers crunch breadsticks, sift rice, squelch spaghetti bolognaise?

What are the foods that I experience on a weekly basis? What are the foods that I experience on special occasions?

Are there any safety concerns that it is important people are aware of with regards to the gustatory stimuli I get to experience?

The texture of experience for _____(name of Sensory Being) by _____(name of person filling in the page) on _____(date observations were made).

Write a list of what my body is in contact with throughout the day (e.g. my clothes, any equipment that touches me as it supports me, any straps or braces that I wear):

Are these things different at different times of the day, or is the texture that I experience throughout the day predominantly the same?

What sorts of textures do I engage with? Do I stroke soft fabric? Do I crunch my fingers into scrunchy paper? Do I press against hard surfaces? Do I show curiosity about flexible materials?

Do I respond with interest to different temperatures? How might I experience different temperatures, e.g. do I get to hold cold metal objects, or feel warmth through a hot water bottle?

What do I reach for? What do I love to touch? (If I cannot reach, think about this question as meaning "what do I reach for with my intention?" It could be that I turn my head a little, or you just see something in my eyes that makes you think I am interested in an object.)

Create a little tally chart for me of different types of touch experiences and note down how many opportunities I get to have them. You could think about different types of materials, e.g. How many wooden things do I get to touch in a day? How many glass? How many metal? How many fabric? How many natural? How many manmade? And so on. Or you could think about types of experience, e.g. How many hot things do I touch in a day? How many cold? How many hard? How many soft? How many sticky? How many liquid?

Are there any types of tactile experience you have spotted I rarely get to have?

Is there anything I do not like to touch?

Does how you present a touch experience to me affect how I respond to it? Do I prefer to touch things gently at first, or firmly? Do I take a while to begin to respond and explore?

Are there any safety concerns that it is important people are aware of with regards to the tactile stimuli I get to experience?

The rock and roll life of _____(name of Sensory Being) by _____ (name of person filling in the page) on _____(date observations were made).

Please think about the movements I experience through a day and through a week. Can you think of occasions when (please give details about any of the following you can identify for me):

I feel pressure on my body? Either to specific parts (for example, someone squeezing my hand) or all over (for example, being submerged in water)?

I feel pull on my body? Think about the types of pull your body would experience as you lifted a heavy bag or if someone were to pull on your arm; when do I feel these things?

I feel my body go up and down?

I feel my body rotate or spin?

I feel vibrations? Where do I feel them?

I receive a massage?

Thinking again about my day-to-day and week-to-week experience, what types of movements do I experience? e.g. Do I feel myself rolling in a wheelchair?

Do I feel myself rolling on the floor? Do I dance? Do I feel myself floating? Are there bumps on a path that I roll along? If I am ambulant, can I run, jump, walk backwards, etc.?

Thinking now about my life as a whole, are there any times, either special or perhaps traumatic, when I experience or have experienced strong proprioceptive or vestibular input? For example, going on a rollercoaster, or being pulled away from a danger. Try to identify times when I've felt extraordinary movement or felt pressure or pull on my body.

[Note: Proprioception is your awareness of where your body is in space; our proprioceptive sensors are in our joints, they note the pressure upon them. Vestibulation is your awareness of movement and balance; our vestibular sensors are in our inner ear, they note movement.]

Have there been any particular proprioceptive or vestibular experiences that I have strongly disliked or liked?